The HUNGRY STUDENT
Vegetarian
Cookbook

The HUNGRY STUDENT

Vegetarian Cookbook

Charlotte Pike

CONTENTS

INTRODUCTION

Feeding yourself well at uni can be a real challenge, and if you're vegetarian, your options might look even more limited. As well as a tight budget, you're probably facing a cramped kitchen, limited equipment and a cooker with a mind of its own! Welcome to student life!

But you don't have to resort to endless takeaways and baked beans, tempting as that might be. With this book and a few essential kitchen tools, you can eat great vegetarian food on a budget every day, whatever the state of your kitchen. Result. If you're cooking for yourself for the first time, this book will show you how to make yummy vegetarian food from scratch quickly and easily. And if you're already a keen cook and want to show off to your friends, you'll find loads of inspiration here too. Vegetarian food isn't just for vegetarians, and this book is full of amazing things to serve to even your meat-eating friends.

Vegetarian food doesn't have to be expensive or difficult to cook. In fact, it's perfect for students because meat is often the most expensive ingredient. So you're already way ahead, budget-wise. Many recipes in this book are cheaper than a takeaway, so you can save your cash for other things. You may need to stock up on a few spices and seasonings, but a little goes a long way, and hopefully you will cook these recipes over and over again. Remember that you can make large batches to eat over a few days, or freeze in portions to pull out when you're too busy (or skint) to do a big shop or spend time cooking.

Making the effort to prepare a good meal that fits around your timetable (and your social life) can be great fun and even stress-busting. When in a black hole of revision, there's nothing like taking some time away from the laptop to tinker in the kitchen. Or crank up some music and cook for your friends – they might even help you wash the dishes...! Whatever your skill level, you *can* cook delicious vegetarian meals from scratch. So add this book to your student survival kit and discover yummy, budget-friendly veggie food and loads of useful tips. Time to get cooking!

KITCHEN KIT

You don't need loads of fancy kitchen equipment to cook great food. Nor do you need everything ready for the first day of term; you can get by with just a few key items while you work out what else will be useful. See what you can share with housemates, too, particularly if you have a small kitchen with limited storage space.

Try to invest a little in any equipment you do buy. It's worth getting a solid frying pan, for example. Very cheap ones cook unevenly, resulting in burning or sticking, but a good one can last for many years. And it may sound like a luxury, but a blender or food processor will pay for itself with homemade dips, soups and smoothies. A stick blender is the most affordable type and comes with a variety of attachments for different jobs. For pricier items like these, see if your parents can help, or look out for bargains in the sales. Here are the main things you'll need:

Large non-stick frying pan or wok

Medium frying pan

Large and small saucepans, with lids

Ovenproof casserole dish with a lid

1.5-litre ovenproof baking dish
(for puds)

Non-stick baking sheet

Large deep roasting tin

20cm square cake tin
(for brownies, etc.)

Mixing bowl or large serving bowl

Microwavable/heatproof bowl
(ideally glass)

Chopping board
(white plastic is most hygienic)

Large and small sharp knives

Kitchen scissors

Wooden spoon(s)

Silicone spatula

Fish slice

Whisk

Can opener

Vegetable peeler

Garlic crusher
(useful but not essential)

Potato masher
(else just use a fork)

Pastry brush
(useful but not essential)

Grater

Pepper grinder

Sieve

Colander

Measuring spoons

Measuring jug

Scales
(electric are most accurate)

Rolling pin
(or use a clean, dry wine bottle)

Wire cooling rack
(or use a clean oven/grill shelf)

Oven gloves
(or use a thick, folded tea towel)

Plastic boxes with lids

Thermos flask

LOVE YOUR OVEN

Every oven is different, so get to know yours. Some run hotter and others run cooler than the temperature they're set to. This doesn't have to be a problem, you just need to get used to it. Follow this advice to get the best from your oven.

* Most modern ovens are electric (with temperatures in degrees centigrade – generally 50–240°C). Look inside to see if yours has a fan at the back (these days, most do). If so, use the temperatures given throughout this book. If you have an electric oven without a fan, add 20°C to the stated cooking temperatures. And just in case you have a gas oven, the recipes also give temperatures in gas marks.

* Always preheat the oven well before you need to put your food in. Most have a thermostat light that comes on when you turn on the oven, and goes out when it reaches the correct temperature. Watch this the first time you use the oven and note how long it takes.

* Keep a close eye on cooking times. Where a recipe gives a range (e.g. 20–30 minutes), always check and test after the minimum (in this case 20 minutes) and, if required, return the food to the oven for some or all of the remaining time. This will ensure your cakes don't burn. It's worth bearing in mind that some ovens are just way out, and so recipes can take much, much longer than they are supposed to. It's useful to make a note next to the recipe of the actual time it ended up taking so you have the information handy for next time.

STOCKING UP YOUR STORE CUPBOARD

You can build up your collection of ingredients as you go along, or maybe ask your parents for a bit of help getting started. Some basics go a long way, so you could even club together with housemates and share. These items will see you through many recipes in this book:

Baking powder

Bicarbonate of soda

Butter (keep in the fridge)

Canned beans

Canned chickpeas

Canned sweetcorn

Canned tomatoes

Caster sugar

Cheese: Cheddar or similar, and vegetarian Parmesan

Coconut milk

Concentrated tomato purée

Couscous

Flour: plain and self-raising

Frozen green vegetables

Garlic

Root ginger

Herbs: thyme, rosemary, basil (fresh or dried)

Honey

Jam

Lemons and limes

Mayonnaise (keep in the fridge)

Milk (keep in the fridge)

Mustard

Noodles

Oats

Oils: sunflower/vegetable and olive oil

Olives (jars or cans are cheapest)

Onions

Pasta and spaghetti

Rice

Salt and pepper

Sauces: tomato, soy, sweet chilli

Spices: ground cinnamon, ground cumin, chilli powder, turmeric, fenugreek

Stock cubes (vegetable)

Yoghurt (natural or Greek is used in cooking)

WATCHING YOUR BUDGET

* **Eating out or buying packet sandwiches** can be a huge drain on your budget, so taking a packed lunch with you to campus, even if only occasionally, can save you a significant amount. Buying takeaway coffees can also be very expensive, so if you love coffee, invest in a cheap cafetière for making good coffee at home – it will soon pay for itself. A Thermos flask is handy for transporting your own tea, coffee or even soup instead of buying it on the go.

* **Before you go shopping, make a list** and plan carefully, based on what you already have in the cupboard and the meals you want to cook. Impulse buying can result in doubling up on items or forgetting a vital ingredient.

* **Shopping around makes a difference.** Be aware much you're paying for every item you buy, and check supermarket websites to see if another sells it more cheaply. Larger, out-of-town supermarkets tend to charge lower prices for many goods than smaller 'city' branches of the same chain. If you can't get to a large branch, then online shopping could be worthwhile – you get the benefit of those lower prices and can also buy some items in bulk (such as washing powder or toilet roll), which can save you cash in the long run. Why not club together with housemates to share the delivery charge?

* **Supermarkets aren't always the best place.** Some ethnic food items – including herbs, spices, rice, noodles, and sauces or flavoured pastes – can be more affordable from Asian or Caribbean grocery stores. And if you have a local market, it's often the cheapest place for fruit, veg, fresh herbs and – if you eat it – even fish (but beware farmers' markets, which sell mainly organic or premium products, at premium prices!).

* **For specialist items, look online.** Whole spices such as cinnamon sticks and vanilla pods tend to be very expensive on the high street, but can be found much cheaper from online suppliers.

* **Keeping it local can save you money** on fresh produce. There are a surprising number of local food cooperatives that sell affordable vegetable boxes. If you live in a city, many community allotments sell seasonal vegetables extremely cheaply, and sometimes even give them away. Often your local independent health food shop can put you in touch with these schemes, or you can search online. Some universities also operate vegetable box schemes, so do ask about this.

* **See if your parents will take you shopping** at the start of term. Stock up on herbs, spices, stock cubes, canned veg and beans, pasta, flour, sugar, etc. With a well-stocked store cupboard, you can pull together so many recipes in this book in a flash, without needing to buy too many extra ingredients.

* **Fresh herbs are a luxury but add a real edge** to home cooking. You could even grow your own on a windowsill – either buy living pots from the supermarket or grow some cuttings taken from the garden at home. Fresh basil, for example, will lift a simple tomato pasta dish and costs next to nothing if you keep a plant.

* **Buy a good-quality sunflower or vegetable oil** for everyday use – for roasting, baking, frying and greasing tins – but spend a little more on a decent bottle of olive oil (extra-virgin if you can stretch to it) for salad dressings and dips. Olive oil has a much nicer flavour, but works best cold.

HOW NOT TO POISON YOUR FRIENDS

Food hygiene might not sound rock-and-roll, but it's really important to get things right so you don't end up ill. Food poisoning is surprisingly common, so here's how to keep yourself and your friends safe.

HYGIENE

* When you first move into a house or halls, the kitchen may not be clean, so it's wise to clean all the surfaces, cupboards, sink and floor with antibacterial cleaner.

* Before touching any food, wash your hands well with hot water and soap. Wash them immediately after handling raw food, and again after cooking.

* Keep on top of kitchen cleaning and don't let the dirty plates pile up. If you need to implement a cleaning rota with your housemates, then do it.

* Wipe up spillages and crumbs straight away, from work surfaces, inside the fridge and on the floor, using a separate mop or cloths for the floor.

* Keep the sink clean and throw away any bits that gather in the plughole every time you wash up.

* Wash up with hot, soapy water. Never wash up using cold water or without washing-up liquid.

* White plastic chopping boards are the cheapest and most hygienic and it's easy to see if they aren't clean. If you eat fish, keep a separate board for this. And if you're living with people who eat meat, insist they prepare it on entirely separate boards and wash all equipment thoroughly and immediately after use.

* Wash fabric cloths and tea towels regularly on a hot wash. Replace sponges or cloths regularly as they can be full of bacteria. If you drop a tea towel on the floor, put it straight in the wash.

* Sweep the floor often and take out the rubbish regularly. If there have been any spillages inside the bin, clean them as soon as you can, using hot water and washing-up liquid or an antibacterial cleaner. Remember that it's never worth economising on bin bags...

COOKING

* If you eat fish, ensure you prepare this separately from any other ingredients and always wash your hands, board and knife really well in hot, soapy water immediately afterwards. If you live with people who cook meat, insist they do the same, both for hygiene and to ensure it doesn't come into contact with your own food.

* Make sure your food is properly cooked through. This particularly applies to fish (if you eat it), which should flake once cooked.

* If you have leftovers, let them cool before wrapping and chilling in the fridge or freezing.

* Make sure food is thoroughly defrosted before reheating it. You can do this in the microwave on a defrost setting, or place the food on a plate, still in its wrapping, and leave in the fridge overnight.

* When reheating leftovers, make sure they are piping hot before serving. You may need to add 1–2 tablespoons of water to stop your food drying out whilst reheating. Only ever reheat food once, as reheating multiple times increases the chance of harmful bacteria growing in the food.

SAFE STORAGE

* Any perishable foods, such as dairy products or fish, should be kept in the fridge, sealed in their original packaging, with cling film or in a food bag. Put these items in the fridge as soon as you get home from shopping and return them to the fridge immediately after use.

* If your housemates have meat in the fridge, ask them to make sure it is extremely well wrapped and kept away from all other produce, ideally on the bottom shelf. If you share a fridge with meat-eaters, it's best to ask for the top shelf to ensure that nothing can drip down onto your food from the shelves above.

* Don't have open packets or uncovered bowls of food in the fridge. Once you open a packet, seal it well, either by putting it in another bag and sealing with a knot or clip or by transferring it to a clean plastic container. Cover bowls of leftovers with cling film. Keep all packets in your cupboard sealed and store biscuits in an airtight box or tin. It will stop food going stale and prevent spillages or, worse, mice.

* Pay attention to use-by dates on food and try to use up everything before then. Discard any fresh ingredients that have been open for a few days.

* If you want to store leftover canned food, always transfer it to a plastic tub with a lid. Never put open tins in the fridge, even if sealed, as they can release chemicals into the food that can cause food poisoning.

CLEVER COOKING

* It may sound obvious, but before you start cooking, check you have all the necessary ingredients and equipment – you don't want to have to rush out to the shops when you're halfway through a recipe!

* Read through the whole method before you begin, so you know exactly what you need to do and when. Allow plenty of time and don't be tempted to rush. Some recipes take time for a reason.

* If you're lacking equipment, be inventive. A clean wine or spirits bottle can be used to roll out pizza dough or pastry. If you don't have a blender, you can roughly mash ingredients with a potato masher or fork and a bit of elbow grease. If you don't have a colander, a sieve works just as well; and a clean oven or grill shelf does the same job as a wire cooling rack.

* If making a cake or pudding, remember that baking is the more scientific side of cooking. Measure all your ingredients accurately and use the specified tin sizes to ensure the recipe works as it should. Never open the oven door until the minimum cooking time has passed – your cake will turn out as flat as a pancake!

* Make the most of your freezer. Freezing sliced bread ensures you'll always have some in for toast or emergency lunches. Make large batches of casseroles or soups and freeze them in separate bagged portions, so you have a stash of instant meals-for-one. Stock up on frozen fruit and vegetables – they are great standby ingredients and much cheaper than fresh equivalents in many cases. Frozen berries are ideal for breakfast smoothies and baking, while frozen green beans, peas and spinach can be thrown into soups, stews and pasta bakes.

KEEPING IT VEGGIE

Avoiding meat isn't always as simple as it sounds. Certain products that might seem suitable for vegetarians can actually contain ingredients derived from animals. Depending on your reasons for not eating meat, this may or may not bother you, but it's best to be aware. Foods where you need to take care are listed below. For more information, visit the Vegetarian Society's website, www.vegsoc.org, and look out for their mark of approval to be sure a product is vegetarian. You'll also find information opposite on veganism.

CHEESE

Not all cheese is vegetarian. Traditional cheese production uses a product called rennet, which comes from cows' stomachs. Nowadays, most mainstream cheeses are made with artificial rennet, which is vegetarian, but it's still best to check the label. But some artisan cheeses (notably Parmesan, Grana Padano and Gorgonzola), are always made with animal rennet – because manufacturers can only legally use these protected names if the cheese is produced in the traditional manner. You can buy vegetarian equivalents, usually labelled 'Parmesan-style hard cheese' or 'Italian hard cheese', while Dolcelatte or Stilton are good vegetarian substitutes for Gorgonzola.

ALCOHOL

Some alcoholic drinks are produced using animal-derived products. Spirits are fine, but many beers, wines and ciders are made using gelatine (see right) or a product derived from fish. Some manufacturers specifically label vegetarian beers and wines, but many don't, and alcoholic drinks don't always have a list of ingredients on the bottle. The best thing is to check online – either on manufacturers' websites or vegetarian forums.

GELATINE

Gelatine is a product derived from cows or pigs, and is present in numerous sweets, including marshmallows and most gummy sweets. It can also be found in chewy cakes and biscuits, margarine, yoghurt, jelly, mousse, and some coloured drinks. It will always be listed on product labels, so check carefully.

E NUMBERS

You might associate E numbers with processed foods and sweets, but in fact an E number can be any kind of additive or preservative, and most things you buy in a supermarket will contain E numbers. E120 and E542 are not suitable for vegetarians. (A much larger number of E numbers are not suitable for vegans: you can check these online.)

MEAT SUBSTITUTES

Some of the recipes in this book call for meat substitutes, such as vegetarian sausages or mince, etc. There are many forms and brands of meat substitute, most of them soya-based, including tofu. Shop around and try different kinds to see what you like. There are also non-soya meat substitutes, such as Quorn, which is derived from a fungus (but note that Quorn, and others, aren't vegan).

EATING FISH

Some people eat fish and shellfish, but no other meat. This is technically called 'pescatarianism'. This book doesn't include fish recipes, but does have a few recipes that feature sauces derived from fish. Use them only if you are okay with eating fish, otherwise just omit.

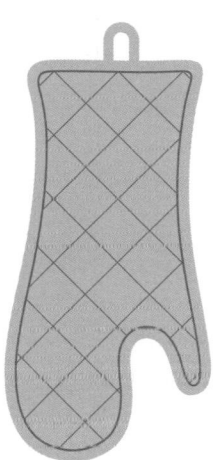

VEGAN DIETS

Vegans avoid not just meat but all animal-derived products: eggs, milk, butter, cheese, etc. Fully vegan recipes in this book are labelled as such, but many other recipes can easily be made vegan by omitting or switching one ingredient: leaving the cheese off pasta, or using dark rather than milk chocolate, for instance. Vegan alternatives to dairy products are widely available, including soya milk, yoghurt and dairy free spreads. One or two ingredients (such as honey) are debatably vegan: if you're cooking for someone else, make sure to check their views.

PASTA

GOES-WITH-EVERYTHING TOMATO SAUCE

Serves: 2 (Vegan)

Although quick and cheap to make, this sauce definitely doesn't compromise on taste! It's a great recipe to keep up your sleeve for a speedy supper. Mix it through pasta, or spread onto a homemade pizza base (see page 116). It can also be frozen, for up to 3 months (defrost fully before use).

2 tsp olive oil

2 garlic cloves, peeled and chopped

400g can chopped tomatoes

1 tsp caster sugar

Salt and pepper

Cooked pasta to serve (optional)

* Warm the olive oil in a small saucepan over a medium heat.

* Add the garlic, stir and cook for 2 minutes until fragrant.

* Add the chopped tomatoes and sugar, and season with salt and pepper. Allow to cook on a medium heat for around 15 minutes until thickened.

* Stir into any cooked and drained pasta or spaghetti, and serve immediately.

CHILLI TOMATO SAUCE

For a feisty version of this sauce, finely chop 1 red chilli (keep the seeds for an added kick, or deseed it first if you don't want it too hot) and add to the pan at the same time as the garlic. Mix with drained pasta and top with chopped fresh parsley, if you fancy.

Tip: Jazz up this sauce with some cooked vegetables, such as broccoli, mushrooms or peppers, or with some fresh or dried herbs, such as basil or rosemary.

MUSHROOM CARBONARA

Serves 3–4

Carbonara is a creamy pasta sauce made with eggs. This vegetarian version includes mushrooms, which add extra taste and texture, instead of the usual bacon. If you've never tried making it before, you should – it's cheap and easy to cook, but indulgent enough to impress your mates. The white wine is optional, so splash some in if you happen to have an open bottle.

400g dried spaghetti

25g butter

200g mushrooms, sliced

3 garlic cloves, peeled and finely chopped

3 tbsp double cream

5 tbsp finely grated vegetarian Parmesan cheese, plus extra to serve (optional)

2 large eggs

3 tbsp dry white wine (optional)

Salt and pepper

* Boil the kettle and fill your largest saucepan with the boiling water. Place on a medium heat and bring back up to the boil, then add a generous pinch of salt and the spaghetti. Cook for the time stated on the packet.

* Meanwhile, melt the butter in a frying pan over a medium heat. Add the mushrooms and garlic and cook for around 4–5 minutes until the mushrooms are golden and the garlic is softened and fragrant. Stir regularly to ensure the garlic does not burn. Remove from the heat.

* Place the cream, cheese and eggs together in a bowl. Season with salt and pepper and whisk together well.

* When the spaghetti is cooked, drain well in a colander. Make sure the saucepan you used to cook the pasta is dry before putting the drained spaghetti back into it. Tip in the cream, cheese and egg mixture and mix well. If you are using wine, add this now.

* Add the cooked mushrooms and garlic and stir in. Allow the egg mixture to begin to set (not over the hob, just in the residual heat from the pasta), for about 1–2 minutes.

* Serve immediately with extra cheese grated on top, if you like.

VEGGIE BOLOGNESE

Serves: 6

Bolognese is a classic pasta sauce that all first-time cooks should learn to make. It works brilliantly with meat-free mince. Although this recipe serves six, you can make the full quantity for yourself and keep leftovers well wrapped in the fridge for 3 days, or divide into portions and freeze. For a speedy dinner, you can then defrost and reheat the sauce in the microwave before adding to cooked pasta.

2 tbsp olive oil

1 large onion,
peeled and finely chopped

1 carrot, peeled and chopped
into 1cm cubes

2 garlic cloves, peeled
and finely chopped

500g vegetarian mince
(see page 15)

4 tbsp concentrated
tomato purée

150ml hot vegetable stock

150ml red wine (optional)

2 x 400g cans chopped tomatoes

1 bay leaf

400g dried spaghetti

Salt and pepper

Finely grated vegetarian
Parmesan cheese or similar,
to serve (optional)

* Heat the olive oil over a medium heat in a very large saucepan. Add the onion, carrot and garlic and cook for about 10 minutes, so that the vegetables soften but do not brown.

* Add the mince and cook over a medium heat until it is brown.

* Add the tomato purée and continue cooking for 2 minutes. Then add the stock and wine, if using, and allow to cook for a further 5 minutes.

* Add the chopped tomatoes, bay leaf and salt and pepper, and stir in well. Bring the heat down to low so the mixture gently simmers. Stir well, and leave to cook for 20–30 minutes until thickened.

* Shortly before you're ready to eat, boil the kettle and fill a large saucepan with the boiling water. Place on a medium heat and bring back up to the boil, then add a generous pinch of salt and the spaghetti. Cook for the time stated on the packet

* When the spaghetti is ready, drain well in a colander. Mix it with the Bolognese sauce, and serve with a sprinkling of grated cheese, if you like.

SUPER TASTY MAC AND CHEESE

Serves: 4

Macaroni cheese is great for lunch and hearty enough for dinner.
Use a strong mature Cheddar, to really pump up the taste. Try the leek
and spinach version below if you also want to squeeze in your greens.

For the filling and topping

400g dried macaroni or pasta

50g vegetarian Parmesan
cheese, finely grated

50g breadcrumbs

For the cheese sauce

700ml milk

50g butter

50g plain flour

200g mature Cheddar cheese,
grated

Salt and pepper

* Preheat the oven to 180°C Fan/Gas Mark 6. Lightly grease the
  base and sides of a large baking dish.

* Boil the kettle and fill your largest saucepan with the boiling
  water. Place on a medium heat and bring back up to the boil,
  then add a generous pinch of salt and the macaroni and cook
  for 2 minutes less than the time stated on the packet. Drain
  well in a colander once cooked.

* Meanwhile, start the cheese sauce. Make sure you have a
  wooden spoon, whisk and the milk measured out in a jug next
  to you. Melt the butter in a large saucepan over a low heat.

* When all the butter is melted, tip in the flour and stir it in quickly
  with the wooden spoon. It will look like a thick paste. Continue
  to stir vigorously for the next couple of minutes until the flour
  and butter paste starts to bubble.

* Pour in the milk a little at a time, whisking vigorously after each
  addition until smooth. When all the milk has been added, the
  sauce should look smooth and glossy. Tip in the grated cheese
  and continue to whisk. Season with salt and plenty of pepper
  and let it bubble gently for 4–5 minutes, whisking continuously.

* Tip the drained macaroni and cheese sauce into the prepared
  baking dish and stir to combine well. Sprinkle the Parmesan
  and breadcrumbs over the top and bake in the oven for 30–40
  minutes until the topping is golden brown and crunchy.

MAC AND CHEESE WITH LEEKS AND SPINACH

Slice 3 medium leeks into 1cm rings and cook with 40g butter
in a frying pan over a medium heat for 20 minutes until soft
but not coloured. In a separate pan, cook 125g frozen spinach
according to the packet, then drain and squeeze out the excess
water. Now follow the recipe above, adding the soft leeks and
drained spinach to the macaroni and cheese sauce in the dish.
Top with the breadcrumbs and cheese and bake as directed.

SPINACH AND PINE NUT LASAGNE

Serves: 4

This is another delicious vegetarian lasagne, with vibrant spinach and crunchy pine nuts. Lasagne is perfect for feeding lots of people – you can easily double the ingredients and cook in a really large baking dish. You can assemble it in advance and pop it in the oven when you are ready.

For the spinach
20g butter

600g fresh spinach leaves

Grated nutmeg

Salt and pepper

For the cheese sauce
300ml milk

15g butter

15g plain flour

100g extra-mature Cheddar or other strong hard cheese, grated

Salt and pepper

To assemble the lasagne
50g pine nuts, toasted for 1–2 minutes in a dry frying pan

200g mozzarella cheese, torn into pieces

4–8 sheets of dried lasagne (depending on dimensions of dish)

75g vegetarian Parmesan, extra-mature Cheddar or other strong hard cheese, grated

* Preheat the oven to 180°C Fan/Gas Mark 6.

* First, wilt the spinach. Melt the butter in a large frying pan over a medium heat. Add the spinach, stir and cook for 1–2 minutes until the leaves are softened. Don't cook for too long or it can turn mushy. Season with salt, pepper and nutmeg.

* Now you need to make the cheese sauce. Make sure you have a wooden spoon, whisk and the milk measured out in a jug next to you. Melt the butter in a large saucepan over a low heat.

* When all the butter is melted, tip in the flour and stir it in quickly with the wooden spoon. It will look like a thick paste. Continue to stir vigorously for the next couple of minutes until the flour and butter paste starts to bubble.

* Pour in the milk a little at a time, whisking well after each addition until smooth. When all the milk has been added, the sauce should look smooth and glossy. Tip in the grated cheese and continue to whisk. Season with salt and plenty of pepper and let it bubble gently for 4–5 minutes, whisking continuously.

* To assemble your lasagne, place a layer of spinach in a large baking dish, then top with a layer of the cheese sauce. Sprinkle over some of the pine nuts and dot some chunks of mozzarella over the top. Cover with pasta sheets. Repeat the process with more layers of spinach, cheese sauce, pine nuts, mozzarella and pasta. Make sure you finish with a layer of pasta at the top, then cover this with the grated cheese.

* Bake in the oven for around 35–45 minutes until the lasagne is bubbling and the cheese on top is golden and melted.

* Leftovers can be kept, well wrapped, in the fridge for 2 days, or frozen in individual portions.

BUTTERNUT SQUASH, RICOTTA AND SAGE LASAGNE

Serves: 4

Homemade lasagne is a million times better than any ready meal. The squash makes this version nice and filling and the ricotta adds a lovely subtle flavour. If you like it really crispy on top, finish under the grill for a few minutes. Lasagne is ideal for feeding a crowd – if necessary, double the recipe and cook in a very large baking dish.

1 really large or 2 small butternut squash, peeled, deseeded and cut into 1cm thick slices

1 tbsp olive oil

250g ricotta

200ml crème fraîche

Few sage leaves, thinly sliced or 1 tsp dried sage

To assemble

8–10 sheets of dried lasagne (depending on dimensions of dish)

50g vegetarian Parmesan cheese, finely grated

* Preheat the oven to 180°C Fan/Gas Mark 6.

* Place the slices of butternut squash in a non-stick roasting tin. Drizzle with olive oil and bake for 30 minutes until soft.

* Cover the bottom of a baking dish with a layer of squash pieces. Dot small spoonfuls of ricotta and crème fraîche over the squash. Sprinkle over a little sage.

* Cover with a layer of pasta sheets and start again, layering up the squash, ricotta and crème fraîche, and pasta. Reserve a little ricotta and crème fraîche for the topping.

* Make sure you have a layer of pasta on the top and then spread this evenly with the remaining ricotta and crème fraîche and sprinkle with the cheese.

* Bake for around 30 minutes until golden and bubbling. Serve with salad on the side.

Tip: Use a small dish if you have one, so that you can build up more layers.

ROASTED MEDITERRANEAN VEGETABLE LASAGNE

Serves: 4–6

This creamy, cheesy lasagne is packed full of delicious, colourful roasted veg. If you like it really crispy on top, finish under the grill for a few minutes. Lasagne is ideal for feeding a crowd – if you need to, you can double the ingredients and cook in a really large baking dish.

For the vegetables

1 aubergine, sliced 1cm thick

2 courgettes, sliced 1cm thick

2 peppers, deseeded and cut into 3cm chunks

200g cherry tomatoes, whole

2 red onions, peeled and sliced 1cm thick

200g chestnut or flat mushrooms

3 tbsp olive oil

Salt and pepper

For the cheese sauce

600ml milk

60g butter

60g plain flour

200g extra-mature Cheddar or other strong hard cheese, grated

Salt and pepper

To assemble

4–8 sheets of dried lasagne (depending on dimensions of dish)

75g vegetarian Parmesan, extra-mature Cheddar or other strong hard cheese, grated

* Preheat the oven to 180°C Fan/Gas Mark 6.

* Start by roasting the vegetables. Lay them out in two large roasting tins and drizzle the oil evenly over the top. Season with salt and pepper. Bake for around 20 minutes until soft.

* Meanwhile, start the cheese sauce. Make sure you have a wooden spoon, whisk and the milk measured out in a jug next to you. Melt the butter in a large saucepan over a low heat.

* When all the butter is melted, tip in the flour and stir it in quickly with the wooden spoon. It will look like a thick paste. Continue to stir vigorously for the next couple of minutes until the paste starts to bubble.

* Pour in the milk a little at a time, whisking well after each addition until smooth. When all the milk has been added, the sauce should look smooth and glossy. Tip in the grated cheese and continue to whisk. Season with salt and plenty of pepper and let it bubble gently for 4–5 minutes, whisking continuously.

* When the vegetables have been roasted and the cheese sauce has been made, you are ready to assemble your lasagne. In a large baking dish, make a layer of the vegetables and then add a layer of the cheese sauce. Cover with pasta sheets and start again, layering up the vegetables, cheese sauce and pasta. Make sure you have a layer of pasta on the top and cover this with the grated cheese for the final layer.

* Bake in the oven for around 30 minutes until it is bubbling and the cheese on the top is golden and melted.

* Leftovers can be kept, well wrapped, in the fridge for 2 days, or frozen in individual portions.

CHEESE AND TOMATO BAKED GNOCCHI

Serves: 4

Gnocchi are little potato dumplings, which are delicious mixed with a sauce and baked in the oven like a pasta bake. Pre-made gnocchi can be bought in supermarkets – they tend to be sold vacuum-packed alongside the fresh pasta.

1 tbsp olive oil

2 garlic cloves,
peeled and chopped

400g can chopped tomatoes

Pinch of caster sugar

500g gnocchi

1 tbsp chopped
fresh basil leaves

125g mozzarella,
cheese torn into pieces

50g vegetarian Parmesan
cheese, finely grated

Salt and pepper

* Preheat the oven to 180°C Fan/Gas Mark 6.

* Warm the oil in a saucepan over a medium heat. Add the garlic and cook gently for a minute or two until fragrant. Don't let it brown.

* Pour in the tomatoes and cook for around 15 minutes until some of the liquid has cooked away. Add the sugar, season with salt and pepper and stir well.

* Meanwhile, boil the kettle and fill a large saucepan with the boiling water. Place on a medium heat and bring back to the boil, then add a pinch of salt and the gnocchi. Cook for the time stated on the packet. Drain well in a colander once cooked.

* Stir the basil leaves into the tomato sauce and add the gnocchi. Stir to coat the gnocchi in the sauce.

* Pour the gnocchi and sauinto a medium-sized ovenproof dish. Dot the mozzarella over the pasta and sprinkle over the Parmesan.

* Bake for 20–30 minutes until the topping is golden and bubbling.

GNOCCHI WITH HOMEMADE GARLIC SAUCE

Serves: 2

Gnocchi aren't technically pasta – these yummy little dumplings are actually made from potato. You can buy them pre-made in the supermarket; they tend to be sold vacuum-packed along with the fresh pasta. They are super-fast to cook and best served with a very simple sauce, such as this delicious garlic and sage butter.

250g gnocchi

35g butter

1 large garlic clove, peeled and chopped

3 large fresh sage leaves, finely chopped

Salt and pepper

40g vegetarian Parmesan cheese, finely grated, to serve

* Boil the kettle and fill a large saucepan with the boiling water. Place on a medium heat and bring back to the boil, then add a pinch of salt and the gnocchi. Cook for the time stated on the packet. Drain well in a colander once cooked.

* Melt the butter in a small saucepan over a medium heat. Add the garlic and sage and cook for just a minute or two until the garlic is fragrant.

* Add the cooked, drained gnocchi to the butter and toss well to coat the gnocchi. Season with salt and pepper.

* Serve immediately with the grated cheese sprinkled on top.

CREAMY GNOCCHI BAKE WITH SPINACH, OLIVES AND WALNUTS

Serves: 4

This delicious creamy bake is full of flavour, with some nice crunch from the walnuts. Use pre-made gnocchi from the supermarket - they are sold in vacuum packs alongside the fresh pasta.

100g frozen spinach

500g gnocchi

4 tbsp double cream

125g mozzarella cheese, torn into pieces

6 pitted black olives, chopped into small pieces

2 tbsp walnut pieces

75g vegetarian Parmesan cheese, finely grated

Salt and pepper

* Preheat the oven to 180°C Fan/Gas Mark 6.

* Cook the frozen spinach according to the packet, then drain and squeeze out all the excess water.

* Boil the kettle and fill a large saucepan with the boiling water. Place on a medium heat and bring back to the boil, then add a pinch of salt and the gnocchi. Cook for the time stated on the packet. Drain well in a colander once cooked.

* Stir the cream, spinach, mozzarella, olives and walnuts into the gnocchi. Season with salt and pepper.

* Tip into a medium-sized baking dish. Sprinkle the Parmesan over the top. Bake for 20–30 minutes until golden and bubbling. Serve immediately.

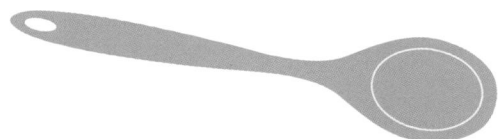

ROASTED VEGETABLE PASTA BAKE

Serves: 4

A pasta bake is the ultimate student dinner – cheap and easy, as well as warm, filling and delicious. Roasted vegetables add lots of flavour, texture and colour to this bake. Use whatever pasta shape you prefer.

2 peppers, deseeded and chopped into 2cm chunks

1 aubergine, chopped into 2cm chunks

1 courgette, chopped into 1cm thick rings

1 tbsp olive oil

400g dried pasta

3½ tbsp red pesto

2 x 125g balls mozzarella cheese, torn into pieces

100g mature Cheddar cheese, grated

Salt and pepper

* Preheat the oven to 180°C Fan/Gas Mark 6.

* Lay all the vegetables out in a large roasting tin (or two).

* Drizzle with olive oil, season with salt and pepper and bake for around 20 minutes until the vegetables are tender.

* Meanwhile, boil the kettle and fill a large saucepan with the boiling water. Place on a medium heat and bring back to the boil, then add a pinch of salt and the pasta. Cook for the time stated on the packet. Drain well in a colander once cooked.

* Tip the pasta into a large baking dish and stir the pesto through evenly. Add the roasted vegetables and stir through. Scatter the mozzarella and Cheddar cheeses evenly over the top.

* Bake the pasta in the oven for 20–30 minutes until the topping is golden and bubbling.

Tip: Leftover roasted vegetables can be used in lots of recipes, so cook extra here if you want some for another day. Supermarkets also sell bags of frozen chargrilled veg that can be used instead, once defrosted.

CHEESY BROCCOLI AND SPINACH PASTA BAKE

Serves: 4

Green veg is a great way to liven up your pasta bake. (Don't worry, it's still got its fair share of cheese!) Use whatever shape of pasta you prefer. Dinner doesn't get cheaper or easier than this.

For the bake
400g dried pasta

200g broccoli, chopped into small florets

1 tsp olive oil

3 garlic cloves, peeled and chopped

1 onion, peeled and chopped

100g fresh spinach leaves

100g mature Cheddar cheese, grated

For the cheese sauce
700ml milk

50g butter

50g plain flour

200g mature Cheddar cheese, grated

Salt and pepper

* Preheat the oven to 200°C Fan/Gas Mark 7.

* Boil the kettle and fill your largest saucepan with the boiling water. Place on a medium heat and bring back to the boil, then add a pinch of salt and the pasta. Cook for the time stated on the packet. Add the broccoli 5 minutes before the end of the pasta cooking time. Drain the pasta and broccoli well in a colander, once cooked.

* Warm the oil in a frying pan over a medium heat. Add the garlic and onion, and cook for about 5 minutes, stirring occasionally, until the onion and garlic are soft but not brown.

* Meanwhile, start the cheese sauce. Make sure you have a wooden spoon, whisk and the milk measured out in a jug next to you. Melt the butter in a large saucepan over a low heat.

* When all the butter is melted, tip in the flour and stir it in quickly with the wooden spoon. It will look like a thick paste. Continue to stir vigorously for the next couple of minutes until the paste starts to bubble.

* Pour in the milk a little at a time, whisking vigorously after each addition until smooth. When all the milk has been added, the sauce should look smooth and glossy. Tip in the grated cheese and continue to whisk. Season with salt and plenty of pepper and let it bubble gently for 4–5 minutes, whisking continuously.

* Stir together the cooked pasta and broccoli, the onion and garlic, the fresh spinach leaves and cheese sauce in a large baking dish. Sprinkle the Cheddar over the top and bake for 20–30 minutes until golden and bubbling.

CREAMY TOMATO PASTA BAKE

Serves: 4

This is a creamy, cheesy pasta bake with a gorgeous topping of sliced fresh tomatoes. It's equally good as comfort food at the end of a long day, or for feeding to friends on a leisurely Sunday afternoon.

For the bake

Knob of butter, for greasing

400g dried macaroni or pasta

125g mozzarella cheese, torn into pieces

2 ripe tomatoes, very thinly sliced

50g vegetarian Parmesan cheese, finely grated

For the cheese sauce

700ml milk

50g butter

50g plain flour

200g mature Cheddar cheese, grated

Salt and pepper

* Preheat the oven to 180°C Fan/Gas Mark 6. Lightly grease the base and sides of a large ovenproof dish with butter.

* Boil the kettle and fill your largest saucepan with the boiling water. Place on a medium heat and bring back to the boil, then add a pinch of salt and the pasta. Cook for the time stated on the packet. Once cooked, drain well in a colander.

* Meanwhile, start the cheese sauce. Make sure you have a wooden spoon, whisk and the milk measured out in a jug next to you. Melt the butter in a large saucepan over a low heat.

* When all the butter is melted, tip in the flour and stir it in quickly with the wooden spoon. It will look like a thick paste. Continue to stir vigorously for the next couple of minutes until the paste starts to bubble.

* Pour in the milk a little at a time, whisking vigorously after each addition until smooth. When all the milk has been added, the sauce should look smooth and glossy. Tip in the grated cheese and continue to whisk. Season with salt and plenty of pepper and let it bubble gently for 4–5 minutes, whisking continuously.

* Place the drained pasta and cheese sauce in the prepared baking dish and stir well to combine evenly. Tuck the pieces of mozzarella cheese into the pasta and lay the tomato slices evenly over the top, overlapping each other. Sprinkle the Parmesan cheese on top.

* Bake in the oven for 30–40 minutes until the topping is golden brown and crunchy.

CHILLI BEAN PASTA BAKE

Serves: 4

This pasta bake has a crunchy breadcrumb topping and a cheeky chilli kick! It uses mostly store-cupboard ingredients, so it's simpler and cheaper to prepare than ever.

400g dried pasta

1 tbsp olive oil

3 garlic cloves, peeled and chopped

2 x 400g cans chopped tomatoes

1 red chilli, finely chopped (deseeded if you don't want it too hot)

1 tsp chopped rosemary, fresh or dried

400g can cannellini beans, drained and rinsed

75g breadcrumbs

75g vegetarian Parmesan cheese, finely grated (optional)

Salt and pepper

* Preheat the oven to 180°C Fan/Gas Mark 6.

* Boil the kettle and fill your largest saucepan with the boiling water. Place on a medium heat and bring back to the boil, then add a pinch of salt and the pasta. Cook for the time stated on the packet. Drain in a colander once cooked.

* Heat the oil in a saucepan over a medium heat. Add the garlic and cook for a minute so that it softens. Add the tomatoes, chilli and rosemary, season with salt and pepper and cook for around 15 minutes until it has thickened.

* Add the cooked pasta and cannellini beans to the sauce and stir to combine well.

* Pour into a baking dish, sprinkle evenly with breadcrumbs and Parmesan, if using, and bake for 20–30 minutes until the topping is crunchy and golden brown. Serve immediately, with a green salad on the side.

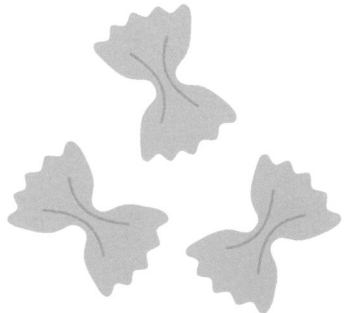

STIR-FRIES, NOODLES AND RICE

GINGER AND ORANGE STIR-FRY

Serves: 2 (Vegan)

A simple, zesty stir-fry made using the simplest of ingredients.

2 tbsp sunflower or
vegetable oil

1 spring onion, thinly sliced

1 garlic clove,
peeled and crushed

3cm piece of fresh root ginger,
peeled and finely grated

400g fresh stir-fry vegetables
(see Tip)

Juice and grated zest
of 1 orange

1 tbsp soy sauce

2 tsp honey

Rice or noodles, to serve
(optional)

* Heat the oil in a wok or frying pan over a high heat until it is very hot. Add the spring onion, garlic and ginger and stir-fry for 30 seconds.

* Add the vegetables and stir-fry for 3–4 minutes until lightly wilted.

* Add the orange juice and zest, soy sauce and honey. Stir through and cook for a further minute so that everything is heated through.

* Serve immediately, with rice or noodles, if you wish.

Tip: A packet of fresh mixed stir-fry vegetables is ideal to use here. Or you can chop up your own: try cabbage, carrot, peppers, beansprouts – whatever you fancy.

SESAME TOFU STIR-FRY

Serves: 2 (Vegan)

Tofu is great for vegetarian meals because it is packed with protein. It has a subtle flavour of its own, but is also very good at absorbing other flavours. Make sure you buy firm tofu, as the 'silken' variety is much softer and will just fall apart in a stir-fry.

1 tbsp sesame seeds

2 tbsp sunflower or vegetable oil

200g firm tofu (smoked or unsmoked is fine), cut into 2cm cubes

2 garlic cloves, peeled and crushed

2 spring onions, thinly sliced

400g fresh stir-fry vegetables (see Tip)

2 tbsp soy sauce, plus a little extra to serve

Rice or noodles, to serve

Tip: A packet of fresh mixed stir-fry vegetables is ideal to use here. Or you can chop up your own: try cabbage, carrot, peppers, beansprouts – whatever you fancy.

* Toast the sesame seeds by placing them in a dry frying pan over a medium heat and cooking for a couple of minutes until you can smell their aroma. Remove from the heat immediately, tip into a bowl and set aside.

* Heat 1 tablespoon of the oil in a wok or large frying pan over a high heat until it is very hot. Add the cubes of tofu and fry on all sides until golden brown and crispy. This should take just under 5 minutes. Remove from the pan and set aside on a sheet of kitchen paper to drain.

* Heat the remaining oil in the pan until very hot, then add the garlic and spring onion and stir-fry for just 30 seconds until they are fragrant. Now, add the vegetables and stir-fry for 3–4 minutes until they are lightly wilted.

* Drizzle with soy sauce, sprinkle with the sesame seeds and stir. Serve immediately with the tofu chunks on top and a little extra soy sauce drizzled over. Accompany with rice or noodles.

CASHEW NUT AND VEGETABLE STIR-FRY

Serves: 2 (Vegan)

This crunchy, fresh-tasting stir-fry is super-quick to cook, so it's wise to get all your ingredients chopped and ready before you begin.

2 tsp sesame seeds

1 tbsp sunflower or vegetable oil

400g stir-fry vegetables of your choice, such as peppers, carrots, onions and broccoli

75g cashew nuts

2 spring onions, finely chopped

1 garlic clove, peeled and crushed

½ red chilli, deseeded and finely chopped

1 tbsp soy sauce, plus a little extra to serve

1 tbsp sesame oil, plus a little extra to serve

Rice or noodles, to serve

* Toast the sesame seeds by placing them in a dry frying pan over a medium heat and cooking for a couple of minutes until you can smell their aroma. Remove from the heat immediately, tip into a bowl and set aside.

* Heat the oil in a wok or large frying pan over a high heat until it is very hot. Add the vegetables and cashew nuts and stir-fry for around 2 minutes until they have started to soften and wilt a little.

* Now, add the spring onion, garlic and chilli and stir-fry for just a couple of minutes until they are cooked.

* Pour over the soy sauce and sesame oil and stir well. Serve immediately with the toasted sesame seeds sprinkled on top and a little extra soy sauce and sesame oil drizzled over. Accompany with rice or noodles.

VEGGIE PAD THAI

Serves: 2

Pad Thai is a yummy mixture of stir-fried flat noodles, vegetables and chilli, with a tangy dressing. It's typically scattered with peanuts, which adds some nice crunch but isn't essential.

2 tbsp sesame seeds

150g dried flat egg noodles

1 tbsp sunflower oil

½ red chilli, finely chopped (deseeded if you don't want it too hot)

1 garlic clove, peeled and crushed

3cm piece of fresh root ginger, peeled and finely grated

3 spring onions, thinly sliced

Handful of beansprouts

½ red pepper, deseeded and thinly sliced

2 tbsp lime juice

1 tbsp soy sauce

1 tsp fish sauce (optional, if you eat fish)

50g peanuts, chopped

1 tbsp chopped fresh coriander

* Toast the sesame seeds by placing them in a dry pan over a medium heat and cooking for a couple of minutes until you can smell their aroma. Remove from the heat immediately, tip into a bowl and set aside.

* Cook the egg noodles according to the packet instructions. Drain well once cooked.

* Heat the oil in a wok or large frying pan over a high heat until very hot. Add the chilli, garlic, ginger and spring onion and stir-fry for a minute or so to soften.

* Add the beansprouts, pepper and cooked noodles and stir-fry for a couple of minutes to heat through.

* Pour over the lime juice, soy sauce and fish sauce (if you're using it) and stir together to combine.

* Once everything's really hot, transfer to plates to serve. Top with the peanuts, toasted sesame seeds and coriander. Serve immediately!

Tip: To get ahead, do all the chopping and grating before you start cooking.

SATAY VEGETABLES

Serves: 2 (Vegan)

Satay sauce is simple to make at home using peanut butter, and will save you a packet on buying a pre-made jar. To make this go even further, add 200g cooked noodles along with the sauce and let them heat through.

1 garlic clove, peeled and crushed

½ tsp ground ginger

2 tbsp peanut butter (your choice of smooth or crunchy)

2 tbsp soy sauce

1 tbsp tomato purée

1 tsp sunflower or vegetable oil

400g fresh stir-fry vegetables, such as beansprouts, peppers, carrots, broccoli, etc.

* Place the garlic, ginger, peanut butter, soy sauce, tomato purée and 2 tablespoons of hot water together in a bowl. Stir vigorously until all the ingredients are blended together.

* Warm the oil in a large frying pan or wok over a high heat until it is very hot. Add the vegetables and stir-fry for a few minutes until they have wilted a little.

* Add the satay sauce and stir-fry for another 2–3 minutes to cook the sauce. Serve immediately.

QUICK CHOW MEIN

Serves: 4

You've probably seen this classic noodle dish on Chinese takeaway menus, but it's also great to cook at home for a main or side dish. Get stuck in and share it with your mates!

250g dried egg noodles

2 tbsp sesame oil

4 spring onions, finely sliced

1 red pepper, deseeded and thinly sliced

200g beansprouts

4 tbsp soy sauce, plus extra to serve

2 tbsp sesame seeds

* Cook the egg noodles according to the packet instructions. Drain well in a colander once cooked.

* Warm half the oil in a wok or large non-stick frying pan over a high heat, until very hot. Add the spring onions and red pepper slices and cook for a minute, stirring vigorously.

* Add the beansprouts and drained noodles. Pour in the soy sauce and remaining oil, and stir-fry for a further 2–3 minutes until everything is heated through. Serve immediately with extra soy sauce and sesame seeds sprinkled on top.

BAKED PUMPKIN RISOTTO

Serves: 4

This tasty risotto is baked in the oven, making it much easier to prepare than a traditional risotto, which involves constant stirring on the hob. Make sure to use risotto rice (see Tip), as other varieties don't work in the same way. If you can't get hold of a pumpkin, butternut squash is a perfectly good alternative.

2 tbsp olive oil

700g pumpkin, peeled, seeds removed and cut into 1cm cubes

30g butter

1 large onion, peeled and finely chopped

2 garlic cloves, peeled and chopped

275g arborio risotto rice (see Tip below)

875ml hot vegetable stock

Salt and pepper

75g vegetarian Parmesan cheese, finely grated

Tip: You need risotto rice, such as arborio, to get the best result here. This type of short-grain rice has lots of floury starch, which makes the risotto thick and creamy.

* Preheat the oven to 180°C Fan/Gas Mark 6.

* Pour the olive oil into a large roasting tin. Add the pumpkin cubes and toss well to ensure each cube is covered in oil. Set aside.

* Melt the butter in a large saucepan over a medium heat. Add the onion and garlic and cook for a couple of minutes until softened and fragrant.

* Add the risotto rice and stir through well.

* Add the hot stock and season with salt and pepper. You may want to go easy on the salt as stock cubes are already salty.

* Bring the risotto to the boil. When it starts to bubble, carefully pour the contents of the pan into a large baking dish.

* Place the risotto and pumpkin in the oven on separate shelves and bake for 12 minutes.

* After 12 minutes, stir the risotto, cover with foil and continue baking the rice and the pumpkin for another 8–10 minutes until the rice is tender.

* Remove the risotto and pumpkin from the oven. Scatter the cubes of pumpkin over the risotto, sprinkle with Parmesan and serve immediately.

BAKED MUSHROOM RISOTTO

Serves: 4

Velvety garlic mushrooms are the perfect addition to this oven-baked risotto, which is much easier than traditional risotto as you don't have to stand and stir it continuously. Make sure you use risotto rice (see Tip on page 45) as other varieties don't work in the same way.

30g butter

1 large onion, peeled and finely chopped

2 garlic cloves, peeled and chopped

250g brown mushrooms, such as field or chestnut, thinly sliced

275g arborio risotto rice (see Tip, page 45)

875ml hot vegetable stock

65g vegetarian Parmesan cheese, finely grated

Salt and pepper

Tip: For a little extra flavour, add 1 teaspoon of rosemary or thyme to the risotto at the same time as you add the stock.

* Preheat the oven to 180°C Fan/Gas Mark 6.

* Melt the butter in a large saucepan over a medium heat. Add the onion and garlic and cook for a couple of minutes until softened and fragrant.

* Add the mushrooms and cook gently for around 10–15 minutes until the mushrooms are slightly golden round the edges and any excess water has cooked away.

* Add the risotto rice and stir through well. Add the hot stock and season with salt and pepper. You may want to go easy on the salt as stock cubes are already salty.

* Bring the risotto up to the boil. When it starts to bubble, carefully transfer the contents of the pan to a large baking dish.

* Bake the risotto for 12 minutes in the oven.

* After 12 minutes, stir the risotto, cover the dish with foil and bake for another 8–10 minutes until the rice is tender.

* Remove the risotto from the oven. Top with Parmesan cheese. Stir well and serve immediately.

CREAMY TOMATO RISOTTO

Serves: 4

Another easy, oven-baked risotto, this time a lovely creamy version complete with sweet cherry tomatoes. Make sure you use risotto rice (see Tip on page 45), as other varieties don't work in the same way.

30g butter

1 large onion, peeled and finely chopped

2 garlic cloves, peeled and chopped

275g arborio risotto rice (see Tip, page 45)

875ml hot vegetable stock

200g cherry tomatoes, halved

2 tsp olive oil

3 tbsp mascarpone

65g vegetarian Parmesan cheese, finely grated

Salt and pepper

* Preheat the oven to 180°C Fan/Gas Mark 6.

* Melt the butter in a large saucepan over a medium heat. Add the onion and garlic and cook for a couple of minutes until softened and fragrant.

* Add the risotto rice and stir through well.

* Add the hot stock and season with salt and pepper. You may want to go easy on the salt as stock cubes are already salty.

* Bring the risotto up to the boil. When it starts to bubble, carefully transfer the contents of the pan to a large baking dish.

* Place the tomatoes in a roasting tin. Drizzle with olive oil and season with salt and pepper.

* Put the risotto and the tomatoes in the oven on separate shelves and bake for 12 minutes, then check if the tomatoes are beginning to soften and brown. If they are, remove from the oven. If not, leave them in there with the risotto for a couple more minutes. Stir the risotto, cover with foil and continue baking for another 8–10 minutes until the rice is tender.

* Remove the risotto from the oven. Stir the mascarpone into the risotto and top with the tomatoes and Parmesan. Stir well and serve immediately.

SPECIAL FRIED RICE

Serves: 4

This wallet-friendly rice dish is packed full of tasty morsels and works well as a meal on its own or is good served with any of the stir-fry recipes in this chapter.

200g long-grain rice

400ml boiling water

Pinch of salt

1 tbsp vegetable oil

3 spring onions, finely chopped

3cm piece of fresh root ginger, peeled and grated

2 garlic cloves, peeled and crushed

1 red chilli, chopped (deseeded if you don't want it too hot)

3 tbsp frozen peas

200g sugar snap peas (optional)

75g salted cashew nuts

2 large eggs, beaten

Soy sauce, to serve

* Place the rice into a large saucepan. Add the boiling water and salt, bring to the boil, cover and cook for the time stated on the packet. Drain well once cooked.

* While the rice is cooking, place the oil into a wok or a large saucepan and heat it over a high heat until it is very hot. Add the spring onions, ginger, garlic, chilli and peas and cook for a minute. Then add the sugar snap peas, if you're using them, and the cashew nuts.

* Add the drained, cooked rice and then pour over the beaten eggs.

* Stir the rice vigorously to distribute the egg evenly and allow it to scramble. Cook for a further 3 minutes to ensure the rice is hot enough before serving, drizzled with soy sauce.

Tip: This recipe can also be made using leftover rice. Take it out of the fridge just before you need it. (Note that eating cold rice can cause food poisoning if it is not kept refrigerated and used within 24 hours).

SOUPS, STEWS
AND CURRIES

ROASTED TOMATO SOUP

Serves: 4 (Vegan)

This soup is a great way to use up tomatoes that are past their best, or any that don't have much flavour – once all the other ingredients have been added, you'll never know.

2 red onions, peeled
and quartered

4 garlic cloves, unpeeled

650g tomatoes
(large or cherry), halved

2 tsp dried basil

2 tbsp olive oil

1 litre hot vegetable stock

Salt and pepper

* Preheat the oven to 180°C Fan/Gas Mark 6.

* Place the onion, garlic and halved tomatoes in a large roasting tin. Sprinkle over the basil, drizzle over the olive oil and season with salt and pepper.

* Bake for 20–30 minutes until the tomatoes are well roasted and the onion is soft. Remove the skins from the garlic cloves and discard.

* Whizz the roasted tomato mixture and stock in a blender, or place in a jug and blitz with a stick blender, until smooth. If you prefer your soup really smooth, you can pass it through a sieve. Gently reheat the soup in a saucepan before serving.

CARROT AND CORIANDER SOUP

Serves: 4 (Vegan)

A steaming bowlful of this mildly spiced soup is nutritious, full of flavour and costs next to nothing to make.

1 tbsp olive oil

1 large onion, peeled
and chopped

450g carrots, peeled and sliced

1 tsp ground coriander

1.2 litres hot vegetable stock

Squeeze of lemon juice

Salt and pepper

* Heat the oil in a large saucepan over a medium heat. Add the onion and carrots and cook until they are softened, but take care they do not brown.

* Add the ground coriander and the stock and bring to the boil. Cover and simmer for around 20 minutes or until the carrot is really tender.

* Whizz in a blender, or blitz with a stick blender, until smooth. Then add the lemon juice and season with salt and pepper. Gently reheat the soup in a saucepan before serving.

SPICY TOMATO AND COUSCOUS SOUP

Serves: 4 (Vegan)

Couscous makes this soup wholesome and filling, but make sure it's simmered for long enough that the grains become soft. The spiciness here is from the harissa, a hot chilli paste that can be bought in jars in the supermarket spice section. It's quite fiery, so add it cautiously. It keeps in the fridge and can be stirred into stews and other soups to add a kick, or is good forked through couscous for flavour.

1 tbsp olive oil

1 large onion, peeled and chopped

Pinch of ground cumin

2 tsp harissa paste

400g can chopped tomatoes

400g can chickpeas, rinsed and drained

60g couscous

500ml hot vegetable stock

Salt and pepper

Handful of fresh coriander leaves, chopped, to serve (optional)

* Heat the oil in a large saucepan over a medium heat. Add the onion and gently cook for 10 minutes or so until it is softened. Watch out, as you don't want it to brown.

* Add the cumin and harissa paste and stir well. Add the tomatoes, chickpeas and couscous, stir again and add the vegetable stock.

* Leave the soup to bubble away for around 15 minutes until it's heated through. The couscous will swell as it cooks.

* Season with salt and pepper, stir through some coriander if you are using it, and serve while hot.

Tip: Leftover soup keeps for a couple of days in the fridge and freezes well in individual portions.

PEA SOUP

Serves: 4

This soup has a lovely fresh flavour and a vivid colour! Frozen peas are best to use here, which is a bonus because they're so cheap. It's a super-quick recipe that can be taken from cupboard to table in under half an hour.

50g butter

1 small onion, peeled and fairly finely chopped

450g frozen peas

750ml hot vegetable stock

1 bay leaf

4 tbsp cream, crème fraîche or full-fat natural yoghurt

Salt and pepper

Tip: Leftover soup keeps for a couple of days in the fridge and freezes well in individual portions.

* Melt the butter in a large saucepan. Add the onion and cook gently over a medium heat for 5–10 minutes until the onion is softened and slightly translucent, but not browned.

* Add the peas and stir well, followed by the stock, bay leaf and salt and pepper. Stir again and leave to bubble away for 10 minutes until the peas are tender.

* Remove the bay leaf and whizz the soup in a blender, or blitz with a stick blender, until smooth.

* Add the cream, crème fraîche or yoghurt, whichever you are using, and stir well.

* Gently reheat the soup in a saucepan. Taste the soup to check the seasoning, add more salt and pepper if you wish, and serve immediately.

* Any leftovers can be kept in the fridge for 2–3 days or, once cooled, frozen in individual portions in freezer bags.

BROCCOLI AND STILTON SOUP

Serves: 4

This thick soup has a lovely strong flavour, and is ideal for using up Stilton or other blue cheese that has been hanging around just a tad too long. It's great served with homemade croutons and crusty bread.

25g butter

1 large onion,
peeled and chopped

1 garlic clove,
peeled and chopped

1 large floury potato (such as Maris Piper, King Edward or Desiree), peeled and chopped into 2cm cubes

1 litre hot vegetable stock

1 large broccoli head,
cut into florets

100g Stilton or other vegetarian blue cheese

Pepper

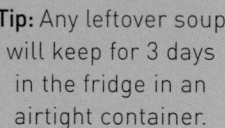

Tip: Any leftover soup will keep for 3 days in the fridge in an airtight container.

* Melt the butter in a large saucepan over a medium heat. Add the onion, garlic and potato and cook for around 10 minutes until the onion and garlic are fragrant.

* Add the vegetable stock and allow to simmer away for a further 10 minutes.

* Add the broccoli and cook for a further 5 minutes until the broccoli and potato are tender.

* Crumble in the cheese, stir well, season with pepper and whizz in a blender, or blitz with a stick blender, until smooth. Gently reheat the soup in a saucepan, add some homemade croutons if desired (see below) and serve.

Homemade croutons

Cut up a thick slice of ciabatta, sourdough or baguette into 2cm chunks. Place 2 tablespoons of olive oil in a frying pan and heat over a medium–high heat. Fry the bread chunks for around 3 minutes until golden and crunchy. Drain on kitchen paper and season with salt and pepper before adding to the soup.

FRENCH ONION SOUP WITH CHEESY TOASTS

Serves: 4

A gorgeous, rich soup that's quick and hearty enough for lunch, but fancy enough to serve as a dinner-party starter if you want to impress your mates. The cheese toasts are popped directly into the soup so the bread becomes soft, chewy and delicious. The wine isn't essential so just throw it in if you happen to have an open bottle; or share the bottle and the soup with friends!

For the soup

40g butter

750g onions, peeled and sliced into 5mm thick rings

2 tbsp plain flour

1.25 litres hot vegetable stock

Small glass (175ml) white wine (optional)

Salt and pepper

For the toasts

8 slices of baguette

100g Gruyère or Cheddar cheese, finely grated

* Melt the butter over a low heat in the largest saucepan you own. Add the sliced onions and allow them to cook gently for 45 minutes. Don't let them burn. This will soften the onions and bring out their sweetness.

* Add the plain flour and stir through the onions. This will thicken the soup.

* Add the hot stock and wine, if using. Season with salt and pepper and leave to bubble away gently for around 15 minutes.

* Meanwhile, get started on the toasts.

* Toast the baguette slices lightly on both sides. Then, top one side with cheese, dividing it evenly among the slices. Grill until the cheese is melted and bubbling.

* Pour the soup into bowls. Place two cheese toasts in each bowl and serve.

FIVE-MINUTE VEGETABLE TOM YUM

Serves: 2 (Vegan)

Tom yum is a popular Thai soup consisting of crisp fresh vegetables simmered quickly in a tangy broth. It's great for when you're feeling under the weather or hungover. Tom yum paste is sold in tubs and jars; look in the spice/condiments aisle or the Asian foods section at the supermarket, or a local Asian grocery store.

500ml hot vegetable stock

2 tsp tom yum paste (see intro)

150g vegetables (try using 75g thinly sliced large flat mushrooms and 75g pak choi)

½ red chilli, finely chopped (deseeded if you don't want it too hot)

2 tsp lime juice

1 tsp fish sauce (optional, if you eat fish)

2 tsp chopped fresh coriander

* Pour the hot vegetable stock into a saucepan. Add the tom yum paste, vegetables and chilli and stir well.

* Simmer for 3–4 minutes until the vegetables are tender.

* Flavour with lime juice, fish sauce, if you're using it, and the fresh coriander.

* Pour into bowls and serve immediately. (This soup doesn't keep particularly well, so is best eaten at once.)

LEEK AND POTATO SOUP

Serves: 4

This thick, creamy soup is a real classic. It's hearty and filling, and perfect for warming your cockles on chilly days.

25g butter

1 leek, thinly sliced

2 onions, peeled and chopped

200g floury potatoes (such as Maris Piper or King Edward), peeled and chopped into cubes

1 litre hot vegetable stock

1 bay leaf

75ml double cream

Salt and pepper

* Melt the butter in a large saucepan over a low heat. Add the leek and onion and cook for around 15 minutes so that they soften, but don't brown.

* Add the potato, stock and bay leaf and allow to bubble away gently for around 20 minutes until the potato is tender.

* Remove the bay leaf, stir in the cream and whizz in a blender, or blitz with a stick blender, until smooth.

* Season with salt and pepper and reheat gently before serving.

Tip: Why not make extra to freeze in individual portions? It can be heated from frozen in the microwave for an emergency lunch.

RED LENTIL SOUP

Serves: 4 (Vegan)

Budget-conscious cooks, listen up! Lentils are your new secret weapon.
Not only are they super-cheap, there are loads of varieties and different
ways to cook with them, and they're guaranteed to fill you up. Here,
they thicken this gently spiced soup, making it a complete meal in a
bowl. This recipe is also suitable for vegans.

1 tbsp olive oil

1 large onion,
peeled and chopped

1 garlic clove,
peeled and chopped

1 celery stick, chopped

1 carrot, peeled and chopped

Pinch of ground cumin

Pinch of ground paprika

200g dried red lentils

400g can chopped tomatoes

500ml hot vegetable stock

Salt and pepper

* Add the olive oil to a large saucepan that has a lid. Place over
  over a medium heat. Add the onion, garlic, celery and carrot
  and cook gently for around 10 minutes until softened.

* Add the spices, lentils, tomatoes and stock. Stir well, cover
  with the lid and allow to bubble away for around 30 minutes
  until the lentils are tender.

* Season with salt and pepper and serve immediately.

VEGGIE JAMBALAYA

Serves: 4 (Vegan)

This is a delicious Caribbean rice stew, a bit like Spanish paella. This vegetarian interpretation uses cheap ingredients and requires very little cooking – it's mostly just a case of leaving it to simmer.

1 tbsp sunflower
or vegetable oil

1 large onion, peeled
and finely chopped

2 garlic cloves, peeled
and finely chopped

½ red chilli, finely chopped
(deseeded if you don't want
it too hot)

3 peppers, deseeded
and cut into 2cm chunks

1 courgette, cut into
1cm thick slices

1 tsp thyme, fresh or dried

1 tsp dried oregano

1 tsp paprika

150g basmati rice

300ml hot vegetable stock

400g can chopped tomatoes

Salt and pepper

* Heat the oil in a large saucepan over a medium heat. Add the onion and cook for around 10 minutes until softened and fragrant.

* Add the garlic and chilli and cook for a couple of minutes until fragrant.

* Add the pepper, courgette, thyme, oregano, paprika and rice and stir together until evenly incorporated.

* Pour in the hot stock and canned tomatoes and season with salt and pepper.

* Allow to bubble away for 30 minutes until the rice is cooked and the vegetables are soft.

Tip: Leftovers will keep for a day in the fridge but make sure to reheat thoroughly before eating. (As cooked rice can cause food poisoning if kept for too long and not reheated properly).

MUSHROOM AND CIDER STROGANOFF

Serves: 4

A stroganoff is a Russian stew, with a rich creamy sauce. Mushrooms and cream were made to go together, so this vegetarian version works really well. The cider adds a tangy edge and stops the cream from becoming sickly. It's gorgeous served with rice and a glass of cider on the side.

25g butter

1 large onion,
peeled and finely sliced

750g mushrooms, cleaned
and cut into quarters

250ml decent-quality cider

200ml double cream

Pinch of dried thyme

Salt and pepper

Rice, to serve

* Melt the butter in a large saucepan over a medium heat. Add the onion and cook for around 10 minutes until softened but not coloured.

* Add the mushrooms and cook for a further 15 minutes until they have softened and shrunk down in size.

* Add the cider, cream and thyme, and season with salt and pepper.

* Allow to bubble away for a further 20 minutes until the sauce has thickened and the mushrooms are tender.

* Serve with some freshly cooked rice.

Tip: You can use any decent-quality cider here, just make sure you don't use a super-strength or flavoured one!

INDIAN SQUASH AND LENTILS

Serves: 4 (Vegan)

This is more of an Indian-spiced casserole than a curry. It's fragrant and filling, with plenty of sauce. You can buy cooked puy lentils in pouches or cans, which is far easier than cooking dried ones.

2 tbsp vegetable or sunflower oil

1 large onion, finely chopped

1 medium butternut squash, peeled, deseeded and cut into 1cm chunks

2 tsp ground ginger

1 tsp each of ground coriander, cumin, cinnamon and garam masala

½ tsp chilli powder

150g pre-cooked puy lentils, from a pouch or can, drained

200ml coconut milk

200ml hot vegetable stock

Salt and pepper

3 handfuls of fresh spinach leaves

Cooked rice and garlic naan breads, to serve

* Warm the oil in a large saucepan over a medium heat. Add the onion and squash and cook for 10 minutes or so, until soft.

* Sprinkle over the ginger, coriander, cumin, cinnamon, garam masala and chilli powder and stir well to combine.

* Add the lentils, coconut milk and stock. Season with salt and pepper. Allow to bubble away for 20 minutes until the squash is tender.

* Add the spinach leaves to the pan and let them wilt, which should take around 3 minutes.

* Serve immediately with rice and garlic naan bread.

AUBERGINE AND CHICKPEA TAGINE

Serves: 4 (Vegan)

A tagine is a rich, intensely spiced stew. It's cooked for a long time over a low heat, so the ingredients absorb loads of flavour and become lovely and tender. This one includes apricots, which gives it some sweetness, too. It's very good served with couscous, fresh coriander leaves and a dollop of natural yoghurt.

1 tsp olive oil

3 garlic cloves, peeled and finely chopped

2.5cm piece of fresh root ginger, peeled and finely grated

1 tsp cumin seeds

2 tsp paprika

2 tsp ground cinnamon

2 tsp tomato purée

400g can chopped tomatoes

400g can chickpeas, drained and rinsed

2 red peppers, deseeded and chopped into 2cm chunks

1 large aubergine, chopped into 2cm chunks

10 dried apricots, chopped

2 tbsp whole almonds

200ml hot vegetable stock

2 tsp honey

4 tsp lemon juice

Salt and pepper

Couscous, to serve

* Warm the oil in a large saucepan over a medium heat. Add the garlic and ginger and cook for a few moments until they are softened and aromatic.

* Add the spices and cook for a further minute, stirring continuously.

* Add the tomato purée, chopped tomatoes, chickpeas, pepper, aubergine, apricots and almonds, then stir all the ingredients together to combine evenly.

* Add the vegetable stock and honey and allow to cook for around 30 minutes or so, stirring every 5 minutes.

* Check the vegetables are tender. If so, you're ready to serve. If not, allow the tagine to cook for another 10 minutes and check again.

* When the tagine is cooked, finish by adding the lemon juice and seasoning with salt and pepper. Serve with couscous.

MOROCCAN VEGETABLE AND HONEY TAGINE

Serves: 4

A tagine is a rich, spiced stew full of intense flavours. This recipe turns humble chickpeas into a delicious feast – cooked slowly with a mix of spices and honey, they absorb loads of gorgeous flavour. If you're serving to friends, it's lovely finished with fresh coriander leaves and a dollop of natural yoghurt.

1 tsp sunflower or vegetable oil

3 garlic cloves, peeled and finely chopped

2.5cm piece of fresh root ginger, peeled and finely grated

1 tsp cumin seeds

2 tsp paprika

2 tsp ground cinnamon

2 tsp tomato purée

400g can chopped tomatoes

400g can chickpeas, drained and rinsed

3 red peppers, deseeded and chopped into 2cm chunks

2 large courgettes, cut into 1cm thick slices

Handful of sultanas (optional)

200ml hot vegetable stock

2 tsp honey

4 tsp lemon juice

Salt and pepper

Couscous, to serve

* Heat the oil in a large saucepan over a medium heat. Add the garlic and ginger and cook for a few minutes until they are softened and aromatic.

* Add the spices and cook for a further minute, stirring continuously.

* Next, add the tomato purée, chopped tomatoes, chickpeas, pepper, courgette and sultanas, if using, and then stir all the ingredients together to combine evenly.

* Add the vegetable stock and honey and allow to cook for around 30 minutes, stirring every 5 minutes.

* Check the vegetables are tender. If so, you're ready to serve. If not, allow the tagine to cook for another 10 minutes and check again.

* When the tagine is cooked, finish by adding the lemon juice and seasoning with salt and pepper. Serve with couscous.

VEGGIE SAUSAGE AND BEAN CASSEROLE

Serves: 4 (Vegan)

Vegetarian sausages are brilliant in this casserole, cooked in a rich tomato sauce with garlic and herbs. The beans really fill it out – a can of mixed beans works well, or you can use your favourite type, such as butter beans, cannellini beans or chickpeas. The red wine isn't essential but does make the sauce richer, so just throw in any you might have left over. Full of flavour, this is perfect on a chilly day.

1 tbsp olive oil

1 red onion, peeled and chopped

2 garlic cloves, peeled and chopped

8 vegetarian sausages

2 x 400g cans chopped tomatoes

400g can mixed beans, rinsed and drained

1 small glass (175ml) red wine (optional)

1 bay leaf

1 tsp sugar

1 tsp thyme, fresh or dried

1 tsp rosemary, fresh or dried

Salt and pepper

Mashed potato and green vegetables to serve

* Warm the oil in a large saucepan over a medium heat. Add the onion and garlic and cook gently for around 10 minutes until softened. Be careful not to let them brown.

* Add the vegetarian sausages and brown them lightly.

* Tip in the tomatoes, beans and wine, if using, add the bay leaf, sugar and herbs, and season with salt and pepper.

* Allow the casserole to bubble away for at least 30 minutes until it has thickened. Serve immediately with some mashed potato and green vegetables.

VEGETABLE AND HALLOUMI STEW

Serves: 4

Halloumi is a firm cheese that can be fried or grilled and still hold its shape. It has quite a salty flavour, so it makes a nice contrast with the slightly sweet tomatoey sauce in this Mediterranean-style stew.

3 tbsp olive oil

1 large onion, peeled and thinly sliced into rings

2 garlic cloves, peeled and chopped

1 orange pepper, deseeded and cut into 2cm chunks

1 yellow pepper, deseeded and cut into 2cm chunks

1 courgette, thinly sliced into rings

400g can chopped tomatoes

1 tsp sugar

200g block of halloumi cheese, drained, patted dry and cut into 1cm thick slices

Salt and pepper

Crusty bread or pitta, to serve

* Heat 2 tablespoons of the olive oil in a large saucepan over a medium heat. Add the onion and garlic and cook gently for 10 minutes or so until softened.

* Add the peppers, courgette, tomatoes and sugar, season with salt and pepper, and allow to bubble away for 45 minutes.

* Meanwhile, cook the halloumi. Heat the remaining oil in a non-stick frying pan over a high heat until hot. Add the slices of halloumi and fry for around 1 minute on each side until browned. Set aside.

* Drop the halloumi into the casserole just 5 minutes before you are ready to serve to heat through.

* Serve hot with crusty bread or pitta.

MUSHROOM CASSEROLE WITH HERBY DUMPLINGS

Serves: 4

This hearty casserole is real comfort food for cold days. Make sure you use vegetable suet for the dumplings as classic suet is made from animal fat. It can be bought in boxes from the supermarket and isn't expensive or complicated to use.

For the casserole

50g butter

2 onions, peeled
and sliced into thin rings

4 garlic cloves,
peeled and chopped

2 carrots, peeled
and chopped into thin slices

2 celery sticks, sliced

750g mushrooms, thickly sliced

1.5 litres hot vegetable stock

1 bay leaf

1 tsp thyme, fresh or dried

Salt and pepper

For the dumplings

100g self-raising flour,
plus extra for your hands

50g vegetable suet

1 tsp herbs, such as fresh
parsley or dried thyme

Salt and pepper

* Melt the butter in a large saucepan over a medium heat. Add the onion, garlic, carrot and celery and cook for around 15 minutes until softened. Take care that they don't brown.

* Add the mushrooms and cook gently for a further 10 minutes.

* Add the stock, bay leaf and thyme, and season with salt and pepper. Stir well and allow to simmer away very gently for at least 30 minutes.

* Meanwhile, make the dumplings. Place the flour, suet, herbs, salt and pepper into a bowl and stir together so that it is all evenly mixed.

* Gradually add 100ml cold water and stir to form a stiff, sticky dough. Flour your hands well and pinch off six pieces of the mixture. Roll into balls using some extra flour to stop them from sticking.

* Drop the dumplings into the casserole 15 minutes before you want to eat, so that they can cook through. Turn them over halfway through the cooking time. Serve with the casserole.

THAI RED COCONUT CURRY

Serves: 2 (Vegan)

Thai curries are incredibly simple to cook, with the ingredients basically left to simmer away in a spicy coconut broth. If this is more than you can eat in one sitting, it can be kept in the fridge and reheated in the microwave.

1 tbsp sunflower oil

2 tbsp Thai red curry paste (double-check the guidance on the jar as brands do vary)

200ml coconut milk

½ butternut squash, deseeded, peeled and cut into 2cm chunks

1 red pepper, deseeded and cut into 1cm thick strips

150g green beans, ends cut off if fresh (frozen are also fine though)

Salt and pepper

Rice, to serve

* Heat the oil in a large saucepan over a medium heat. Add the curry paste and spread it out evenly in the oil. Allow it to cook for 1–2 minutes while stirring continuously.

* Add the coconut milk and butternut squash, then cover the pan and let the curry bubble gently for 15 minutes or so.

* After this time, uncover, stir well and add the pepper and beans. Cook for another 5 minutes or so until the vegetables are cooked through. If you are using frozen green beans, you may need to cook these for another 2 minutes or so until the beans are tender.

* Season the curry with salt and pepper and serve with rice.

BUTTERNUT SQUASH AND PEA CURRY

Serves: 4 (Vegan)

A rich, colourful, coconutty curry, which is easy to make from scratch and much healthier than using a sauce from a jar! Don't be put off by the fenugreek and turmeric – you can find them in the supermarket spice section or even leave them out if you must. If you like cooking curries or Indian food, though, they are a good investment for your store cupboard.

2 tsp ground fenugreek

2 tsp ground turmeric

2 tsp cumin seeds

2 tsp coriander seeds

2 tsp chilli powder

2 tbsp sunflower oil

1 onion, peeled and cut into thin rings

4 garlic cloves, peeled and chopped

6cm chunk of fresh root ginger, peeled and finely grated

1 medium butternut squash, peeled and cut into 1cm cubes

250g frozen peas

400g can chopped tomatoes

400ml can coconut milk

Pilau rice and naan bread, to serve

* Place the spices into a non-stick frying pan and dry-fry them for a minute or two on a medium heat until you can smell them starting to cook. Remove from the heat so the spices don't burn and transfer them in a bowl to cool slightly.

* Add the oil to a large saucepan and heat gently over a low heat. Add the onion, garlic and ginger and cook gently for 10 minutes until the onions are soft. Don't allow any of the ingredients to brown: keep the heat low.

* Meanwhile, grind the cooled spices into a powder using a pestle and mortar or coffee grinder. If you don't have either, simply place the spices in a plastic food bag and crush them using a rolling pin or the bottom of a wine bottle.

* Add the squash, frozen peas and ground spices to the pan and cook for a further 2–3 minutes, still on a gentle heat.

* Now add the chopped tomatoes and coconut milk and cook for another 10 minutes or so until the sauce has thickened and the squash is tender.

* Serve with rice and naan bread. This curry will keep for up to 3 days in the fridge if you have leftovers. It also freezes well.

CURRY IN A HURRY

Serves: 4 (Vegan)

A delicious vegetable curry that will be on the table quicker than you can say 'takeaway'! If you're not in a rush, it also works well cooked more slowly, so leave to bubble for 30 minutes once you've added the stock. Garam masala is a blend of spices that saves on buying lots of different jars. It appears in many curry recipes so is a good investment if you enjoy Indian food.

1 large cauliflower, cut into small florets

2 tbsp sunflower or vegetable oil

2 large onions, peeled and finely sliced into rings

4 garlic cloves, peeled and finely chopped

4cm piece of fresh root ginger, peeled and finely grated

Pinch of chilli powder

2 tsp each of ground coriander, cumin and garam masala

1 medium aubergine, cut into 1cm cubes

400g can chopped tomatoes

200ml hot vegetable stock

Salt

Rice and naan bread, to serve

* Start by cooking the cauliflower until just tender by boiling for 5 minutes or cooking for a few minutes in the microwave with a couple of tablespoons of water.

* While the cauliflower is cooking, heat the oil in a large saucepan over a medium heat. Add the onion, garlic and ginger and cook for around 5 minutes until they are softened and fragrant.

* Add the spices to the pan and stir well. Add the aubergine, tomatoes and stock and cook for around 10 minutes until the aubergine is tender.

* Add the salt and cooked cauliflower and stir well. Cook for another couple of minutes until the cauliflower is heated through and serve immediately with rice and naan bread.

Tip: Scatter with chopped fresh coriander to serve, if you have some.

VEGETABLE GUMBO WITH CORNBREAD

Serves: 4 (Vegan)

Gumbo is a spicy stew made with okra. The okra are best kept whole rather than cut open, or they can become slimy. Cornbread is an American classic served with stews. This recipe makes nine squares.

For the cornbread

Sunflower oil, for greasing

65g self-raising flour

2 tsp baking powder

220g fine-ground polenta or fine cornmeal

1 tsp salt

2 tsp caster sugar

75g butter, melted

275ml milk

50ml natural full-fat yoghurt

2 large eggs, beaten

For the gumbo

2 tbsp sunflower oil

1 onion, peeled and chopped

2 garlic cloves, peeled and chopped

1–2 red or green chillies, deseeded and finely chopped

1 tsp thyme, fresh or dried

1 tsp cayenne pepper

1 tsp dried oregano

1 bay leaf

2 peppers, deseeded and cut into large chunks

1 courgette, sliced 1cm thick

300g okra, left whole

400g can chopped tomatoes

300ml hot vegetable stock

* Preheat the oven to 200°C Fan/Gas Mark 7. Grease and line a 20cm square baking tin with non-stick baking paper.

* Sift the flour and baking powder through a sieve into a large bowl, add the polenta or cornmeal, salt and sugar, and stir together well.

* Pour in the melted butter, milk and yoghurt and stir in well. Finally, add the beaten eggs and stir to combine.

* Pour the batter into the prepared tin and bake for 18–22 minutes until it is lightly golden, soft and springy to the touch. Leave to cool in the tin for 20 minutes to firm up.

* Meanwhile, make the gumbo. Warm the oil in a large frying pan over a medium heat. Add the onion and garlic and cook gently for around 10 minutes. You want to soften them and make sure they don't colour. If they start to brown, turn the heat down.

* Add the chilli, thyme, cayenne, oregano and bay leaf and stir well. Next, add the prepared vegetables, okra, canned tomatoes and hot stock. Stir again to ensure everything is well combined.

* Allow the gumbo to bubble away gently for 20–30 minutes until the vegetables are tender.

* Cut the cornbread into slices and enjoy with the gumbo.

SALADS, VEGGIES AND SIDES

BEETROOT, CARROT AND ORANGE SALAD

Serves: 1 (Vegan)

This colourful, crunchy salad will really brighten up your plate! The grated beetroot and carrot can be prepared in advance and will keep in the fridge for a day or two, but don't add the orange and dressing until just before you want to eat or the salad will go soggy.

½ **fresh beetroot, peeled and grated**

1 **carrot, peeled and grated**

1 **orange, cut into segments, ideally with the pith removed**

2 **tsp olive oil**

2 **tsp orange juice**

Salt and pepper

* Place the grated beetroot, carrot and orange together into a large bowl and mix together well.

* Whisk the olive oil, orange juice, salt and pepper together in a small jug or bowl. Pour over the salad and stir well. Serve immediately.

Tip: Be careful when preparing the beetroot as it can stain the work surface.

WALDORF SALAD

Serves: 1 (Vegan)

A fresh, crunchy salad of apple, celery and walnuts, so-called because it was first served at the Waldorf Hotel in New York, over 100 years ago.

2 celery sticks, thinly sliced

Handful of grapes, halved

½ eating apple, cored and cut into 1cm cubes (skin on or off)

Small handful of walnut pieces

Small handful of sultanas

2 tsp mayonnaise

Lettuce or bread, to serve

* Place all the ingredients into a bowl and mix well.

* Serve immediately on its own, with some lettuce or with some bread on the side.

GREEK SALAD

Serves: 2

This classic salad is best made with the freshest ingredients you can lay your hands on. Fresh olives can be pricey, so if you're on a budget you can use olives from a can or jar, which are much more affordable.

10 cherry tomatoes, halved

10cm piece of cucumber, peeled and cut into 1cm chunks

¼ red onion, peeled and very thinly sliced

50g feta cheese, crumbled

2 tbsp pitted black olives

1 tbsp extra virgin olive oil

1 tsp red wine vinegar

Salt and pepper

Fresh bread, to serve

* Place the tomatoes, cucumber, onion, feta and olives into a bowl.

* Pour the oil into a small jug or cup, add the red wine vinegar, season with salt and pepper and whisk together well.

* Pour the dressing over the salad and stir to coat.

* Serve the salad with some fresh bread.

GRILLED HALLOUMI WITH LEMON CAPER DRESSING

Serves: 2

This light salad is lovely in summer and ideal for serving at barbecues. Halloumi is a firm cheese that can be fried or grilled and still holds its shape. It has quite a salty flavour, so the lemony dressing is a nice contrast here.

1 tbsp plain flour

1 halloumi cheese (approximately 225–250g), cut lengthways into 1cm slices

3 tbsp olive oil

Juice of ½ lemon

1 tsp capers

Handful of fresh coriander leaves (optional)

100g rocket leaves

Salt and pepper

* Sprinkle the flour on a plate and season well with salt and pepper. Take the slices of halloumi and coat them with flour on both sides.

* Heat 1 tablespoon of the oil in a small frying pan on a medium temperature. Allow the olive oil to get hot, which will take a minute or so, and then place the floured slices of halloumi into the pan.

* Fry the halloumi for 1 minute on each side until it is golden brown and feels soft.

* Make the lemon dressing by whisking the remaining 2 tablespoons of olive oil with the lemon juice, capers, salt and pepper and fresh coriander, if you are using it.

* Scatter the rocket leaves onto your plates. Top with the hot halloumi and pour the lemon dressing over the halloumi to serve.

MALAYSIAN PEANUT SALAD

Serves: 1 (Vegan)

A healthy salad of fresh, crunchy vegetables with a gorgeous nutty sauce. If you like satay, you'll also like this. Choose whatever vegetables you prefer.

1 tbsp crunchy peanut butter

1 tbsp orange juice

1 tbsp soy sauce

100g mixed stir-fry vegetables, including carrot, beansprouts, peppers, cabbage and baby corn

* Place the peanut butter, orange juice and soy sauce together in a small jug or cup and whisk together well. It won't be entirely smooth, but don't worry.

* Place the vegetables into a bowl and pour over the dressing. Toss together so that the vegetables are evenly coated in the dressing and enjoy immediately.

STUFFED MUSHROOMS WITH FETA AND RED ONIONS

Serves: 2

These mushrooms are packed full of flavour and are great for lunch served with some crusty bread and salad. They also make a brilliant starter if you're trying to impress friends.

1 tbsp olive oil

1 small red onion, peeled and thinly sliced into rings

½ tsp caster sugar

2 large field or portobello mushrooms

50g feta cheese, crumbled

2 pinches of thyme, fresh or dried

1 tsp lemon juice

Salt and pepper

* Preheat the oven to 180°C Fan/Gas Mark 6.

* Warm 1 teaspoon of the olive oil in a small frying pan over a medium heat. Add the onion and allow it to cook gently for around 15 minutes until tender and translucent looking. Sprinkle with the sugar and stir well to combine.

* Lay the mushrooms, stalk side upwards, in a roasting tin or ovenproof dish. Spread the softened onion evenly around the stalk on the dark brown gills of each mushroom. Sprinkle over the feta cheese and season with salt and pepper, thyme and lemon juice.

* Bake for around 15 minutes until the feta cheese is browned and the mushrooms are tender and juicy.

* Serve immediately.

BREADED MOZZARELLA WITH TOMATO SALSA

Serves: 2

Soft mozzarella is amazing covered in breadcrumbs and fried until hot and melting. Yes, it's a bit indulgent, but you can make yourself feel less naughty by serving it with this fresh crunchy homemade salsa and a big green salad.

For the mozzarella

3 tbsp plain flour

1 large egg, beaten

3 tbsp dried breadcrumbs

125g mozzarella cheese, cut into 1cm thick slices

1 tbsp olive oil

Salt and pepper

For the salsa

10 cherry tomatoes, halved

¼ small red onion, peeled and thinly sliced

½ red pepper, deseeded and cut into small cubes

1 tbsp olive oil

Salt and pepper

* Sprinkle the flour on a small plate and season with salt and pepper. Place the beaten egg in a shallow bowl and the breadcrumbs on another plate.

* Take one slice of mozzarella at a time and coat with the flour, then egg, then breadcrumbs, in that order. Set to one side once covered in breadcrumbs.

* When all the slices of cheese have been covered in breadcrumbs, heat the oil in a non-stick frying pan over a medium to high heat. Fry the mozzarella for about 2 minutes on each side, until golden brown.

* Make the salsa by mixing the tomatoes, onion and pepper together in a bowl. Drizzle over the oil, season with salt and pepper and stir well.

* Place the fried mozzarella onto plates and serve with plenty of salsa and salad on the side. Enjoy immediately while the cheese is hot and the salsa fresh.

Tip: Mozzarella cheese stays fresh unopened in the fridge for a while, so you can keep the ingredients on hand to make this in minutes.

TURKISH BULGHUR WHEAT AND VEGETABLES

Serves: 4 as a side or 2 generously as a main (Vegan)

Bulghur wheat is similar to couscous and is usually sold alongside lentils and rice. This salad is very transportable if you want to take it in a tub for lunch on campus, or it's excellent served at a barbecue. It's a good way to use up leftover roasted vegetables, or you can buy bags of frozen chargrilled Mediterranean veg in larger supermarkets.

1 courgette, cut into 1cm thick rings

1 pepper, deseeded and cut into 2cm chunks

1 aubergine, cut into 2cm chunks

2 tbsp olive oil

150g bulghur wheat

2 spring onions, thinly sliced

Pinch of ground cumin

Pinch of paprika

1 tbsp lemon juice

2 tbsp finely chopped fresh herbs, such as parsley, coriander and mint

Salt and pepper

* Preheat the oven to 180°C Fan/Gas Mark 6.

* Place the vegetables in a roasting tin and drizzle over 1 tablespoon of the olive oil. Roast in the oven for 20–25 minutes until they're really soft.

* Meanwhile, cook the bulghur wheat according to the packet instructions. Drain well once cooked, if necessary.

* Place the cooked vegetables and bulghur wheat into a bowl. Add all the remaining ingredients and the rest of the oil, stir well and serve immediately, either still warm or cold. If you're making the salad in advance, however, don't dress it with the oil and lemon juice until you are ready to serve.

STUFFED PEPPERS

Pepper halves are a delicious vehicle for all kinds of lovely fillings. They're simple and quick to fill, and depending on what you use to stuff them, usually make quite a healthy meal. Enjoy them warm or cold. Here are three delicious ideas for fillings.

STUFFED PEPPERS WITH COUSCOUS

Serves: 2 (Vegan)

2 peppers, halved and deseeded
80g couscous
80ml boiling water
6 cherry tomatoes, halved
3 olives, pitted and halved
Some chopped fresh herbs, such as basil or parsley
Drizzle of olive oil
Salt and pepper

Non-stick baking sheet

* Preheat the oven to 180°C Fan/Gas Mark 6.

* Lay the prepared pepper halves on a non-stick baking sheet.

* Place the couscous into a small bowl. Pour over the boiling water and cover with cling film. Leave for 5 minutes. Remove the cling film and fluff up the couscous using a fork.

* Season the couscous with salt and pepper and tip in the tomatoes, olives and herbs. Stir well and then spoon into the pepper halves. Drizzle over some olive oil.

* Bake for 20–30 minutes until the peppers are soft.

STUFFED PEPPERS WITH TOMATOES AND GARLIC

Serves: 2 (Vegan)

2 peppers, halved and deseeded

6 cherry tomatoes, halved

4 garlic cloves, skin on

Drizzle of olive oil

Couple of fresh basil leaves (optional)

Salt and pepper

Non-stick baking sheet

* Preheat the oven to 180°C Fan/Gas Mark 6.

* Lay the prepared pepper halves out on a non-stick baking sheet.

* Fill the pepper halves with the cherry tomatoes and garlic. Drizzle over some olive oil and season with salt and pepper. If you are using basil leaves, tuck a leaf or two in among the tomatoes so it will flavour them but won't burn.

* Bake for 20–30 minutes until the peppers are soft.

STUFFED PEPPERS WITH PESTO RICE

Serves: 2

2 peppers, halved and deseeded

90g cold cooked rice (or 50g uncooked rice)

1 tbsp basil pesto

2 spring onions, finely chopped

40g cheese, such as vegetarian Parmesan or mature Cheddar, grated

Non-stick baking sheet

* Preheat the oven to 180°C Fan/Gas Mark 6.

* Lay the prepared pepper halves on a non-stick baking sheet.

* If using uncooked rice, place in a large saucepan with boiling water and salt, bring to the boil, cover and cook for the time stated on the packet. Drain well once cooked.

* When the rice is cooked, stir in the pesto and spring onions. Mix until the pesto is evenly distributed through the rice.

* Spoon the rice into the peppers. Top with cheese and bake for 20–30 minutes until the peppers are soft and the cheese is melted and bubbling.

STUFFED TOMATOES WITH COUSCOUS AND FETA

Serves: 2

These make a simple healthy meal that's great for lunch with a big salad. They can also be eaten cold the following day.

2 large beef tomatoes

50g couscous

2 spring onions, finely chopped

50g feta cheese, crumbled

2 tbsp chopped fresh herbs, such as basil or parsley

Salt and pepper

Green salad to serve

Large baking sheet

* Preheat the oven to 180°C Fan/Gas Mark 6.

* Cut the tops off the tomatoes and scoop out the seeds using a spoon. Discard the seeds and then place the hollowed-out tomatoes onto a large baking sheet.

* Cook the couscous according to the packet instructions. Once cooked, fluff up the grains using a fork. Add the spring onion, feta and herbs, and season with salt and pepper. Stir together well so all the ingredients are evenly mixed.

* Spoon the couscous and feta into the tomatoes and bake for 20 minutes or so until heated through. The top of the couscous will brown a little.

* Serve hot or cold with a green salad.

GRILLED VEGETABLE KEBABS

Serves: 4 (Vegan)

These tasty kebabs are great served on a mound of fluffy couscous. They're also particularly good chargrilled on the barbecue.

2 garlic cloves,
peeled and crushed

5 tbsp olive oil

Juice of ½ lemon

1 small aubergine,
cut into 2cm chunks

1 courgette, cut into
1cm thick slices

3 peppers, deseeded
and cut into 2cm chunks

Salt and pepper

4 skewers

* Place the garlic, olive oil and lemon juice into a bowl and season with salt and pepper.

* Add the vegetable chunks, stir well, cover with cling film and chill in the fridge for at least an hour.

* When you are ready to cook the kebabs, preheat the grill to a high temperature.

* Take four skewers and thread the vegetable chunks evenly on to the skewers. Place on a grill pan.

* Grill for 12–15 minutes, turning them over halfway through the time, until the vegetables are tender and very slightly charred around the edges.

Tip: If you are using wooden skewers, soak them in water for at least 30 minutes before use so they don't burn while cooking.

TUNISIAN-SPICED PEPPERS WITH A FRIED EGG

Serves: 2

A really unusual dish of spiced, soft vegetables topped with a fried egg. The perfect egg has a crispy white and a lovely runny yolk.

1 tbsp olive oil

1 tsp ground cumin

Pinch of ground cinnamon

1 red and 1 green pepper, deseeded and chopped into 2cm chunks

400g can chopped tomatoes

2 large eggs

Handful of fresh coriander leaves, chopped

Salt and pepper

* Warm half the oil in a non-stick frying pan over a medium heat. Add the spices and fry in the oil for 1 minute until you can start to smell them cooking.

* Tip in the peppers and cook for 5 minutes to soften.

* Add the canned tomatoes, season with salt and pepper and leave it to cook for 20 minutes until the peppers are completely soft and the sauce is thickened.

* When the vegetables are cooked, heat the remaining oil in a separate frying pan. Crack in the eggs and fry until the white is solid, which should take around 2–3 minutes.

* Serve the vegetables topped with a fried egg and sprinkle over the fresh coriander.

SPICED SPINACH WITH BLACK EYE BEANS

Serves: 4

A nutritious dish that's great served on its own or as a side. Garam masala is a powdered blend of spices that saves having to buy loads of different jars. It's a good investment if you enjoy spiced or Asian food.

400g fresh or frozen spinach

2 tbsp sunflower
or vegetable oil

1 onion, peeled
and finely chopped

1 garlic clove, peeled
and chopped

1 red chilli, deseeded
and finely chopped

3cm piece of fresh root ginger,
peeled and finely grated

2 tsp garam masala

400g can black eye beans,
rinsed and drained

3 tbsp coconut milk

3 tbsp double cream

Salt and pepper

* If using frozen spinach, defrost fully before you begin, and press in a sieve to remove all excess water.

* Heat the oil in a saucepan (use one with a lid) over a medium heat. Add the onion, garlic, chilli and ginger and cook for a couple of minutes until softened and fragrant.

* Add the garam masala and stir well.

* Add the spinach leaves and black eye beans, stir well and cover the pan with the lid. Cook for 3–4 minutes. If you're using fresh spinach, it will have begun to wilt.

* Pour in the coconut milk and cream and stir through. Season with salt and pepper and cook for a minute or two more, to ensure that everything is heated through. Serve immediately as this dish doesn't keep very well.

Tip: If you've opened a whole can of coconut milk, store the rest in an airtight container in the fridge for 2 days. It can be used for other recipes in this book, including curries, porridge, ice cream and rice pudding.

BAKED COURGETTES WITH FETA AND MINT

Serves: 2

These are simple to put together but look really lovely. They're great for lunch or excellent at barbecues.

2 large courgettes,
sliced in half lengthways

2 tsp olive oil

40g feta cheese, crumbled

2 tsp chopped fresh mint leaves

Salt and pepper

Non-stick baking sheet

* Preheat the oven to 180°C Fan/Gas Mark 6.

* Lay the courgette halves out, cut side facing up, on a non-stick baking sheet.

* Mix the oil, cheese, mint, and salt and pepper together in a bowl to combine evenly. Spoon the mixture over the cut side of the courgettes, running down the entire length.

* Bake for 15–25 minutes until the courgettes are tender and the feta is golden.

* Serve hot or cold.

JACKET
POTATOES
AND TOPPINGS

OVEN-BAKED JACKET POTATO

Serves: 1 (Vegan)

The humble jacket potato makes a great standby meal, as well as being one of the best comfort foods known to man! Keep a potato or two in the cupboard and you will always be able to rustle up dinner. Oven-baked jacket potatoes are especially good because of their crispy skins. Add whatever fillings or toppings you fancy (see pages 102–05 for ideas).

1 baking potato (check the variety you buy is suitable for baking)

2 large pinches of salt

> **Tip:** Keep raw potatoes in a dark cupboard, not out on the counter or in a fruit bowl or they will start to sprout. They also shouldn't be kept in the fridge as the moist environment makes them go bad much faster.

* Preheat the oven to 220°C Fan/Gas Mark 9.

* With a sharp knife prick your potato five or six times all over. This will prevent it from potentially exploding in the oven!

* Wash your potato well and shake off the excess water.

* While the potato skin is still slightly damp, sprinkle the salt over the potato and rub it all over the skin.

* Bake the potato directly on the oven shelf for around 50–75 minutes, depending on the size of your potato.

* Test if the potato is done by sticking a sharp knife into it to see how soft it feels. The knife should easily slip into the potato when it is cooked enough. The skin should also feel crisp to the touch. If it's not quite cooked, bake for a further 10 minutes and test again.

* Serve immediately with your topping of choice (see the following pages for ideas).

MICROWAVED JACKET POTATO

Serves: 1 (Vegan)

If you're in a hurry, jacket potatoes can also be done in the microwave. They won't have a crispy skin like oven-baked ones, but they'll be ready in a fraction of the time. Add whatever fillings or toppings you fancy (see pages 102-05 for ideas).

1 baking potato (check the variety you buy is suitable for baking)

* Wash your potato well and dry thoroughly.

* With a sharp knife prick your potato five or six times all over. This will prevent it from potentially exploding in the microwave!

* Place the potato on a microwaveable plate and cook for 4 minutes on High for a small potato, or 6 minutes on High for a large potato.

* Turn the potato over and cook, again on High, for another 4–6 minutes, depending on the size. A small potato may take 8 minutes in total, a large potato may take 12 minutes.

* Test if the potato is done by sticking a sharp knife into it to see how soft it feels. The knife should easily slip into the potato when it is cooked enough. If it's not quite cooked, microwave for a further 2 minutes and test again.

* Serve immediately with your topping of choice (see the following pages for ideas).

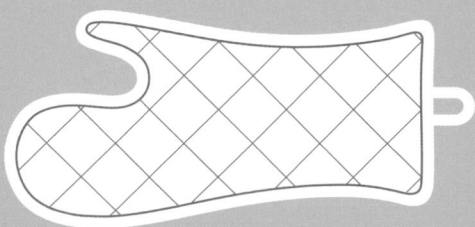

JACKET POTATO TOPPINGS

CHEDDAR, APPLE AND CELERY

Serves: 1

30g Cheddar cheese, grated

1 small eating apple, cored and chopped into small chunks

1 celery stick, chopped into small chunks

1 tsp mayonnaise

1 freshly cooked jacket potato (see pages 100–101)

* Place all the ingredients in a bowl. Stir together and spoon on top of a cooked jacket potato, cut in half. Serve immediately.

CREAMY MUSHROOMS WITH HERBS

Serves: 1

20g butter

1 garlic clove, finely chopped

1 large mushroom or 3–4 small mushrooms, sliced 5mm thick

2 tbsp cream, full-fat crème fraîche or full-fat cream cheese

1 tsp chopped fresh herbs, such as chives or parsley

Salt and pepper

1 freshly cooked jacket potato (see pages 100–101)

* Melt the butter in a small saucepan over a medium heat.

* Add the chopped garlic and cook for a minute or two until you can smell the garlic cooking.

* Add the mushrooms and allow them to cook for 10 minutes or so until soft. Pour away any excess water that has come out of the mushrooms.

* Add the cream, crème fraîche or cream cheese and the herbs, and stir well to combine with the mushrooms. Season with salt and pepper and serve immediately on top of the jacket potato.

CHEESE AND SPRING ONION

Serves: 1

1 freshly cooked jacket potato
(see pages 100–101)

40g mature Cheddar, grated

25ml soured cream (optional)

1 spring onion, thinly sliced

Salt and pepper

* Preheat the oven to 200°C Fan/Gas Mark 7. (If you've used the oven to bake your potato, you can just leave it on and turn it down once the potato is removed.)

* Once the potato is cooked, cut it in half and scoop out the flesh from the skin. Place the fluffy potato flesh into a bowl. Add half the cheese along with the soured cream, if using, and spring onion, season with salt and pepper and mix well.

* Spoon the potato mixture back into the skins. Sprinkle the remaining cheese on top.

* Bake in the oven for 20 minutes until golden and the cheese has melted.

BRIE AND CRANBERRIES

Serves: 1

1 freshly cooked jacket potato
(see pages 100–101)

2–4 thick slices of Brie,
depending on taste

1–2 tsp dried cranberries

* Cut the cooked jacket potato in half.

* Lay the slices of Brie on top of the potato. Sprinkle over the cranberries, adding as many as you fancy, and enjoy immediately.

HOUMOUS AND ROASTED PEPPERS

Serves: 1 (Vegan)

½ red pepper, deseeded
and cut into 1cm strips

1 tbsp olive oil

1 tbsp houmous
(shop-bought or see page 122)

Salt and pepper

1 freshly cooked jacket potato
(see pages 100–101)

* If you're using the oven to bake your potato, you can start making the peppers about 20 minutes before it is cooked. Otherwise, preheat the oven to 180°C Fan/Gas Mark 6.

* Lay the pepper out in a roasting tin and drizzle the oil evenly over the top. Season with salt and pepper. Bake for around 20 minutes until soft.

* Cut open your jacket potato and top with the houmous and roasted peppers.

GOAT'S CHEESE, GRAPES AND WALNUTS

Serves: 1

50g goat's cheese, crumbled
or cut into small pieces

8 red or white grapes, halved

2 heaped tsp chopped walnuts

1 tsp mayonnaise

1 freshly cooked jacket potato
(see pages 100–101)

* Place the goat's cheese, grapes, walnuts and mayonnaise in a bowl and stir together.

* Cut the cooked jacket potato in half and spoon the mixture over the top. Serve immediately.

EASY
DINNERS

MUSHROOM OMELETTE

Serves: 1–2

Perfect for when you've got better places to be than the kitchen, an omelette might be the fastest dinner known to man! Choose the most flavoursome mushrooms you can here (i.e. steer clear of white button mushrooms).

Large knob of butter

100g chestnut mushrooms, sliced

4 large eggs

25g mature Cheddar, grated (optional)

Salt and pepper

* Melt the butter in a small non-stick frying pan over a medium heat.

* Add the mushrooms to the pan and cook gently for around 15 minutes until they are softened and have shrunk.

* Meanwhile, whisk the eggs in a bowl. Add the cheese, if you are using it , season with salt and pepper, and whisk again well.

* Pour the egg mixture into the pan over the mushrooms and swirl it around so it evenly covers the base.

* Allow the omelette to cook for 2 minutes or so on a medium heat. During this time, run a spatula around the edges to ensure the egg doesn't stick, and swirl the pan every minute or so to allow any liquid egg to travel to the edges and cook. Make sure the hob isn't too hot or the bottom of the omelette will burn.

* The omelette is ready to turn when there is only a small amount of liquid egg left on top. Very carefully place a large plate over the pan. Make sure you wear oven gloves. Flip the pan and plate very quickly so that the omelette is now on the plate, then slide it back into the pan, cooked-side up.

* Cook for a further 2–3 minutes until the omelette is cooked through. Check this by cutting into the centre with a sharp knife to see if the middle is still runny. If it's not properly set, allow to cook for a further minute and check again.

* Serve immediately or cool and wrap in foil. It will keep for 2 days in the fridge if wrapped well.

SPINACH OMELETTE

Serves: 2

A standby dinner for when time is short and the fridge is almost bare.
With just these few simple ingredients, you won't go hungry!

15g butter

150g fresh spinach leaves, washed

4 large eggs

Pinch of ground nutmeg (optional)

Salt and pepper

* Melt the butter in a small non-stick frying pan on a medium heat.

* Add the spinach leaves and let them wilt in the butter. This should take 2–3 minutes.

* Crack the eggs into a bowl and season with salt and pepper. Add the nutmeg, if you're using it. Whisk together well. Tip the wilted spinach into the egg mixture and stir to distribute the spinach throughout.

* Pour the egg mixture into the pan and swirl it around so it evenly covers the base.

* Allow the omelette to cook for 3 minutes or so on a medium heat. During this time, run a spatula around the edges to ensure the egg does not stick, and swirl the pan every minute or so to allow any liquid egg to travel to the edges and cook. Make sure the hob isn't too hot or the bottom of the omelette will burn.

* The omelette is ready to turn when there is only a small amount of liquid egg left on top. Very carefully place a large plate over the pan. Make sure you wear oven gloves. Flip the pan and plate very quickly so that the omelette is now on the plate, then slide it back into the pan, cooked-side up.

* Cook for a further 2–3 minutes until the omelette is cooked through. Check this by cutting into the centre with a sharp knife to see if the middle is still runny. If it's not properly set, allow to cook for a further minute and check again.

* Serve immediately or cool and wrap in foil. It will keep for 2 days in the fridge if wrapped well.

ROOT VEGETABLE FRITTATA

Serves: 2

A frittata is a kind of chunky omelette that is cooked in a frying pan. It's a brilliant standby meal and this version is a great way to use up any root vegetables that are lurking in the bottom of your fridge.

35g butter

1 carrot, peeled and cut into 5mm thick slices lengthways

1 parsnip, peeled and cut into 5mm thick slices lengthways

4 small waxy new potatoes, cut into 5mm thick slices lengthways

1 red onion, thinly sliced into rings

4 large eggs

Salt and pepper

Tip: You can vary the vegetables in this recipe depending on what you need to use up! Different veg might need to cook for more or less time – just make sure it is tender before adding the eggs.

* Melt the butter in a non-stick frying pan over a low to medium heat. Add the carrot, parsnip, potato and onion, and cook gently for around 10 minutes until golden and tender.

* Crack the eggs into a bowl and season with salt and pepper. Whisk together well.

* Pour the egg mixture into the pan around the vegetables and swirl it around so it evenly covers the base.

* Allow the frittata to cook for 3 minutes or so on a medium heat. During this time, run a spatula around the edges to ensure the egg does not stick, and swirl the pan every minute or so to allow any liquid egg to travel to the edges and cook. Make sure the hob isn't too hot or the bottom of the frittata will burn.

* The frittata is ready to turn when there is only a small amount of liquid egg left on top. Very carefully place a large plate over the pan. Make sure you wear oven gloves. Flip the pan and plate very quickly so that the frittata is now on the plate, then slide it back into the pan, cooked-side up.

* Cook for a further 2–3 minutes until the frittata is cooked through. Check this by cutting into the centre with a sharp knife to see if the middle is still runny. If it's not properly set, allow to cook for a further minute and check again.

* Serve immediately or cool and wrap in foil. It will keep for 2 days in the fridge if wrapped well.

FETA AND TOMATO FRITTATA

Serves: 2

Feta cheese keeps in an unopened pack for several weeks in the fridge, so it is a useful standby ingredient. It's great in this frittata.

Large knob of butter
4 large eggs
50g feta cheese, crumbled
6 cherry tomatoes, halved
Salt and pepper

* Melt the butter in a small non-stick frying pan on a medium heat.

* Meanwhile, whisk the eggs in a bowl, season with salt and pepper and whisk again well.

* Pour the egg mixture into the pan and swirl it around so it evenly covers the base. Scatter the cheese and tomatoes evenly over the egg mixture.

* Allow the frittata to cook for 4 minutes or so on a medium heat. During this time, run a spatula around the edges to ensure the egg does not stick, and swirl the pan every minute or so to allow any liquid egg to travel to the edges and cook. Make sure the hob isn't too hot or the bottom of the frittata will burn.

* The frittata is ready to turn when there is only a small amount of liquid egg left on top. Very carefully place a large plate over the pan. Make sure you wear oven gloves. Flip the pan and plate very quickly so that the frittata is now on the plate, then slide it back into the pan, cooked-side up.

* Cook for a further 2–3 minutes until the frittata is cooked through. Check this by cutting into the centre with a sharp knife to see if the middle is still runny. If it's not properly set, allow to cook for a further minute and check again.

* Serve immediately or cool and wrap in foil. It will keep for 2 days in the fridge if wrapped well.

SPANISH TORTILLA

Serves: 2 generously

A traditional Spanish tortilla is a thick omelette made with potatoes. This one also packs a punch with onion and red pepper. If you have any slices left over, they're great cold for a packed lunch.

1 tbsp olive oil

1 medium potato,
peeled and cut into 1cm cubes

1 small onion, peeled
and finely chopped

½ red pepper, deseeded
and cut into 1cm cubes

6 large eggs

Salt and pepper

* Warm the olive oil in a large non-stick frying pan on a medium heat. Add the cubes of potato, and cook for 10 minutes until browned and softened. Add the onion and pepper and cook for another 10 minutes until softened.

* Place the eggs in a bowl and whisk well. Season with salt and pepper. Pour the egg mixture into the pan over the potato, onion and red pepper.

* Allow to cook for 5 minutes or so on a medium heat. During this time, run a spatula around the edges to ensure the egg does not stick, and swirl the pan every minute or so to allow any liquid egg to travel to the edges and cook. Make sure the hob is not too hot or the bottom of the tortilla will burn.

* The tortilla is ready to turn when there is only a small amount of liquid egg left on top. Very carefully place a large plate over the pan. Make sure you wear oven gloves. Flip the pan and plate very quickly so that the tortilla is now on the plate, then slide it back into the pan, cooked-side up.

* Cook for a further 3–5 minutes until the tortilla is cooked through. Check this by cutting into the centre with a sharp knife to see if the middle is still runny. If it's not properly set, allow to cook for a further 2 minutes and check again.

* Serve immediately or cool and wrap in foil. It will keep for 2 days in the fridge if wrapped well.

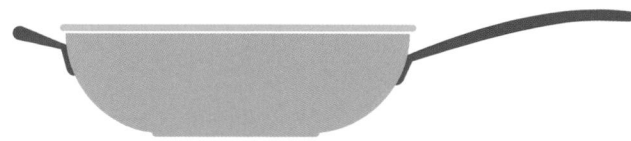

INSTANT PIZZA

Serves: 1

This cheat's pizza can be thrown together in minutes by simply loading your favourite pizza toppings onto crusty bread. Perfect as a hot, cheesy, late-night snack!

½ small baguette, ciabatta loaf or an English muffin

1 tbsp tomato purée

Pinch of dried oregano or mixed herbs

60g grated Cheddar or sliced mozzarella cheese

* Preheat the grill to a medium hot heat.

* Place the bread on the grill pan and toast lightly on both sides. Remove from the grill and spread the cut side with tomato purée. Sprinkle over the herbs and top with whichever cheese you are using.

* Return to the grill and cook until the cheese has melted and is bubbling.

Tip: You can adapt this recipe to use whatever ingredients you have in. Try adding olives, spinach or rocket leaves underneath the cheese if you fancy extra flavour.

HOMEMADE PIZZA

Makes: 1 large pizza (serves 1–2)

A homemade pizza is infinitely tastier and cheaper than a takeaway or frozen one from the supermarket. If you're cooking for a crowd, simply multiply the recipe accordingly to make extra bases, then add your choice of toppings. See pages 117–20 for topping ideas.

200g strong white bread flour

½ tsp salt

⅓ tsp fast-action dried yeast

¼ tsp sugar

125ml warm water

2 tsp olive oil

3 tbsp tomato sauce (page 18)

60g mozzarella cheese, torn into strips

Toppings of your choice

Large baking sheet

Tip: Pizza dough freezes very well, so you can make extra bases and freeze them once shaped, then defrost and bake another time.

* Sift the flour and salt through a sieve into a large mixing bowl and add the yeast and sugar. Add the warm water (it should be body temperature) and 1 teaspoon of the oil and mix until the ingredients come together into a sticky dough.

* Turn out the dough onto a floured work surface and knead gently for a couple of minutes until the dough starts to feel smoother.

* Place the dough back into the bowl, cover with cling film and a clean tea towel and leave in a warm place to rise for an hour. This can be near a warm oven or in the sunlight by a window. The dough should almost double in size.

* Preheat the oven to 220°C Fan/Gas Mark 9. Grease a large baking sheet lightly with the remaining 1 teaspoon of oil.

* Turn out the dough onto a lightly floured surface again and knead gently for around 5 minutes until it feels smooth, elastic and less sticky. Shape the dough into a circle as thick or thin as you like.

* Transfer the dough to the baking sheet, spread with tomato sauce and mozzarella cheese and add your favourite toppings.

* Bake for 10 minutes, then slide the pizza off the baking sheet onto the oven shelf and bake for another 2–3 minutes until the base is golden and crispy and the cheese is melted.

* Serve immediately. Any leftovers are great in a packed lunch.

GARLIC AND THYME MUSHROOM PIZZA BIANCA

Serves: 1–2

Meaning 'white pizza' in Italian, this topping uses crème fraîche instead of tomato purée.

10g butter

1 garlic clove, peeled and finely chopped

75g chestnut or large flat mushrooms, thinly sliced

½ tsp dried thyme

4 tsp crème fraîche

60g mozzarella cheese, torn up

25g vegetarian Parmesan cheese, finely grated

Salt and pepper

* Melt the butter in a small frying pan over a low heat. Add the garlic and cook for a couple of minutes until fragrant. Add the mushrooms and thyme and season with salt and pepper. Cook for around 15 minutes until the mushrooms are tender.

* When the pizza dough is shaped and ready on the baking sheet, spread the crème fraîche evenly over the dough. Scatter the cooked mushrooms over the top, dot with mozzarella and sprinkle with the Parmesan.

* Bake in the oven following the instructions on page 116.

TAHINI AND ROASTED VEGETABLES PIZZA

Serves: 1–2 (Vegan)

Tahini is a sesame seed paste with a distinctive flavour. Find it near spices in the supermarket. It's great topped with your choice of roasted veg (see page 129), such as peppers, courgettes, tomatoes, aubergine and red onion. This topping option is suitable for vegans.

1 tbsp tahini

100g roasted vegetables

* When the pizza dough is shaped and ready on the baking sheet, spread the tahini evenly over the dough. Scatter the roasted vegetables over the base.

* Bake in the oven following the instructions on page 116.

FIORENTINA PIZZA

Serves: 1–2

Topped with mozzarella, spinach and black olives, this delicious pizza also has a fried egg in the middle! It's best to use a very fresh egg here so that the white holds together well.

1 tsp olive oil

75g spinach leaves

3 tbsp tomato sauce
(see page 18)

60g mozzarella cheese,
torn into pieces

6 black olives, pitted

1 large egg

* Warm the oil in a frying pan over a medium heat. Add the spinach leaves and let them wilt, which should take just a minute or two.

* When the pizza dough is shaped and ready on the baking sheet, spread the tomato sauce evenly over the dough. Scatter the wilted spinach, mozzarella cheese and olives evenly over the pizza base.

* Crack the egg into the centre of the pizza.

* Bake in the oven following the instructions on page 116, but see Tip.

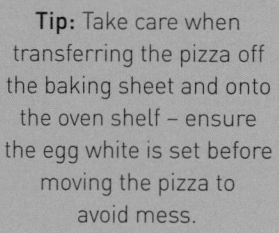

Tip: Take care when transferring the pizza off the baking sheet and onto the oven shelf – ensure the egg white is set before moving the pizza to avoid mess.

GOAT'S CHEESE AND CARAMELISED RED ONION PIZZA

Serves: 1–2

With lovely gooey onions and creamy goat's cheese, this pizza has the perfect balance of sweet and savoury.

1 tsp olive oil

1 small red onion, peeled and finely sliced into rings

1 tsp caster sugar

3 tbsp tomato sauce (see page 18)

60g goat's cheese, broken into small chunks or crumbled, depending on how soft it is

Salt and pepper

* Warm the oil in a small frying pan over a low heat. Add the onion, season with salt and pepper and sprinkle with the sugar. Cook for around 20 minutes until the onions are soft and almost translucent.

* When the pizza dough is shaped and ready on the baking sheet, spread the tomato sauce evenly over the dough. Scatter the onion and goat's cheese over the pizza base.

* Bake in the oven following the instructions on page 116.

COURGETTE, TOMATO AND GARLIC PIZZA

Serves: 1–2

A good one for garlic lovers, follow the tomato sauce recipe on page 18 but add an extra clove of garlic to really up the flavour. The subtle tomato and courgette let the garlic do the talking here!

3 tbsp tomato sauce (see page 18)

60g mozzarella cheese, torn into pieces

½ courgette, cut into 5mm thick slices

* When the pizza dough is shaped and ready on the baking sheet, spread the tomato sauce evenly over the dough. Lay the mozzarella cheese and courgette slices evenly over the pizza base.

* Bake in the oven following the instructions on page 116.

BEAN BURGERS

Makes: 2 really large burgers

Transform a simple can of mixed beans into flavoursome homemade burgers! These taste better than anything shop-bought and are very easy to put together, especially if you have a food processor. Serve either with a big salad, or in buns with melted cheese.

4 tbsp olive oil

½ small red onion,
peeled and finely chopped

1 garlic clove,
peeled and crushed

½ small red chilli,
deseeded and finely chopped

400g can mixed beans,
rinsed and drained

Pinch of ground cumin

Pinch of chilli powder

1 tsp ground coriander

1 tbsp fresh coriander
or parsley, finely chopped

1 large egg

100g dried breadcrumbs

Salt and pepper

2 burger buns, sauces
and, salad to serve

* Heat 1 tablespoon of the oil in a small frying pan. Add the onion, garlic and chilli and cook for a couple of minutes until softened and fragrant.

* If you have a food processor, place the onion, garlic, chilli, beans, spices, herbs and salt and pepper together into the processor and blitz until nearly smooth. Otherwise, mash the ingredients well using a potato masher.

* Form the mixture into two large burgers. Place on a plate, cover with cling film and chill for at least an hour to firm up.

* Preheat the oven to 200°C Fan/Gas Mark 7.

* Break the egg into a shallow bowl and beat with a fork. Scatter the breadcrumbs on a plate. Heat the remaining oil in a non-stick frying pan over a medium heat.

* Remove the burgers from the fridge and cover them all over in the egg, then the breadcrumbs, and place them in the pan.

* Cook over a medium heat for around 10 minutes on each side to brown. Transfer the burgers to the oven and bake for 15–20 minutes until hot throughout.

* Serve in burger buns with your choice of sauces and salad.

HOMEMADE FALAFEL

Makes: 8–10 falafel (Vegan)

Making falafel yourself costs a lot less than buying pre-made ones, and they tend to stay fresh for longer. Eat as a quick wholesome lunch with salad, pitta and houmous (shop-bought or see below) or serve on top of the bulghur wheat salad on page 88.

1 small red onion,
peeled and roughly chopped

1 garlic clove, peeled

½ red chilli, deseeded

1 tsp ground cumin

1 tsp ground coriander

400g can chickpeas,
drained, rinsed and dried

4 tsp plain flour

50g dried breadcrumbs

6 tsp fresh herbs,
such as coriander or parsley,
finely chopped

100ml sunflower
or vegetable oil

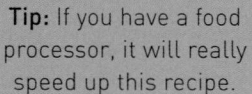

Tip: If you have a food processor, it will really speed up this recipe.

* If using a food processor, place the onion, garlic and chilli into the machine and blitz until very finely chopped. If you don't have a processor, just chop the onion, garlic and chilli finely.

* Add the spices, chickpeas, flour, breadcrumbs and herbs and blitz until very finely chopped. Again, if you don't have a processor, mash together well using a potato masher.

* Bring the mixture together and squash to form golf ball-sized falafel. Place onto a plate, cover with cling film and refrigerate for at least an hour.

* When you are ready to cook the falafel, pour the oil into a large frying pan so that it is around 1cm deep (you may need a little more or less than 100ml).

* Heat the oil and then add the falafel. Fry until they are a deep golden brown on all sides, taking care when turning as they can be fragile. It should take around 5 minutes to fry the falafel.

* Once cooked, place on a plate covered with a couple of sheets of kitchen paper to drain.

* Allow to cool a little before serving as they will be very hot. They keep very well for a couple of days in the fridge.

HOMEMADE HOUMOUS

Serves: 2–3

Drain a 400g can of chickpeas and place in a food processor or blender (or mash by hand) with 1 tablespoon of lemon juice, a finely chopped garlic clove, 1 teaspoon of tahini paste and 30ml extra-virgin olive oil. Season with salt and pepper and blitz for a minute or two to a smooth purée. Serve with an extra drizzle of olive oil on top, if you like. This houmous will keep for 5 days in the fridge in a well-sealed plastic container.

VEGGIE BEAN CHILLI

Serves: 4 (Vegan)

This hearty chilli works brilliantly with vegetarian mince and you can simply adjust the amount of chilli powder according to how much spice you like. It's great served with rice, jacket potatoes or garlic bread. If it's just you eating, you could still make the full batch and freeze the leftovers for instant dinners on other days.

1 tbsp olive oil

1 onion, peeled
and finely chopped

3 garlic cloves,
peeled and chopped

500g vegetarian mince

1 tsp ground cumin

1 tsp ground coriander

1 tsp ground cinnamon

1 tsp hot chilli powder

400g can red kidney beans,
drained and rinsed

2 x 400g cans chopped tomatoes

3 tbsp tomato purée

1 tbsp soy sauce

Salt and pepper

Rice, to serve

* Warm the oil in a large frying pan on a medium heat. Add the onion and garlic and cook for 5–10 minutes until they are softened. Watch that the pan does not get too hot as you do not want the onions and garlic to brown.

* Add the vegetarian mince. Add the cumin, coriander, cinnamon and chilli powder and stir well.

* Add the kidney beans and tomatoes, including the juice in the can, and finally the tomato purée and soy sauce. Stir well and season with salt and pepper.

* Leave the chilli to bubble away gently for a minimum of 20 minutes before serving with rice.

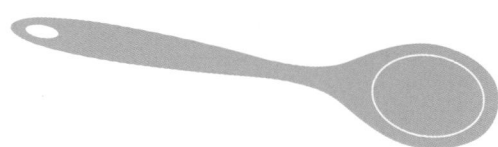

LENTIL SHEPHERD'S PIE

Serves: 4

Lentils really do the job in this hearty veggie shepherd's pie that's just as good and filling as the original. The red wine isn't essential but does make the pie nice and rich, so take the opportunity if you have an open bottle. Topped with gorgeous cheesy mash, this is a great Sunday or cold-weather feast.

900g floury potatoes, peeled and cut into chunks

1 tbsp olive oil

1 large onion, peeled and finely chopped

2 garlic cloves, peeled and finely chopped

1 carrot, peeled and cut into small cubes

2 celery sticks, finely chopped

400g can green lentils, rinsed and drained

350g mushrooms, cut into quarters

400g can chopped tomatoes

200ml red wine (optional)

2 tsp fresh thyme

25g butter

100g mature Cheddar cheese, grated

300g fresh spinach leaves

Salt and pepper

Green salad, to serve

* Place the potatoes in a large pan of salted water. Bring to the boil and cook the potatoes for around 15–20 minutes until tender. Drain well once cooked.

* Meanwhile, warm the oil in a large saucepan over a medium heat. Add the onion, garlic, carrot and celery and cook gently for around 15 minutes until everything is softened, but not browned.

* Add the lentils, mushrooms, tomatoes, wine (if using) and thyme, and stir well. Allow the pie mixture to bubble away for another 10 minutes.

* Preheat the oven to 200°C Fan/Gas Mark 7.

* Return the drained cooked potatoes to the saucepan (making sure there is no residual water in there) and add the butter and cheese. Season with salt and pepper and mash together well. Set aside.

* Add the spinach leaves to the pie mixture, season with salt and pepper and stir together well. Tip into the bottom of a baking dish.

* Cover with an even layer of mashed potato, placing it over the pie in spoonfuls and smoothing out with the back of the spoon.

* Bake for around 30–45 minutes until the filling is bubbling and the topping is golden. Serve immediately, with a green salad.

AUBERGINE AND GOAT'S CHEESE STACK

Serves: 1

A great alternative to a veggie burger, this delicious vegetable stack is perfect for times when you don't want to spend ages cooking. Serve with your favourite sauce or relish.

3 thick slices of aubergine

Drizzle of olive oil

1 large burger bun or crusty roll

1 thick slice of goat's cheese (or enough to spread on the bun)

Couple of thin slices of red onion

Thick slice of tomato

Some lettuce leaves, such as rocket or spinach

2 tsp tomato chutney

Salt and pepper

* Preheat the grill to a medium–hot heat.

* Lay the slices of aubergine on a plate. Drizzle with the olive oil and season with salt and pepper. Rub the oil and seasoning into both sides of the aubergine.

* Place the aubergine slices on the grill pan and grill for 3–4 minutes on each side until the aubergine is softened and golden. Remove from the grill once cooked and set aside.

* Split the burger bun or roll in half and toast the cut side lightly under the grill.

* Place the bottom half of the bun on a plate and spread with the goat's cheese. Top with the onion, tomato and lettuce leaves, and finally lay the aubergine slices on top.

* Spread the tomato chutney on the bun lid and place on top. Enjoy immediately.

ROASTED VEGETABLE AND GOAT'S CHEESE TART

Serves: 4

This simple tart bypasses the complicated bits by using shop-bought pastry. Simply unroll it and off you go. These roasted veggies are also great for other recipes (such as the pizza on page 117) so why not make extra to keep in the fridge for a couple of days?

1 red onion, peeled and chopped into quarters

1 red, orange or yellow pepper, deseeded and chopped into 2cm chunks

2 large tomatoes, cut into quarters

1 courgette, cut into 1cm thick slices

1 tbsp olive oil

1 tsp dried mixed herbs or fresh parsley, rosemary or thyme (optional)

375g packet of ready-rolled puff pastry, fridge-cold

1 tbsp basil pesto

1 tbsp milk

100g goat's cheese

Salt and pepper

Large baking sheet
Non-stick baking paper

* Preheat the oven to 180°C/Gas Mark 6 and line a large baking sheet with non-stick baking paper.

* Place the prepared vegetables in a large mixing bowl. Pour over the olive oil, season with salt and pepper and add the herbs, if you are using any, and stir well to coat the vegetables in oil and seasoning.

* Tip the vegetables out into a large roasting tin and bake for 25–35 minutes until the vegetables are soft and slightly crisp around the edges.

* Unroll the puff pastry onto the prepared baking sheet. If it does not fit, just halve it and make two tarts on two sheets.

* Use a sharp knife to score a border within the pastry rectangle, scoring parallel to the edge of the pastry but roughly 2–3cm in from it.

* Spread the pesto inside the inner rectangle you have just marked out. Brush the milk around the outer border of the pastry, either using a pastry brush, or just dabbing it on with your fingers.

* Top the pesto with the roasted vegetables, crumble over the goat's cheese and bake for 18–20 minutes.

* When the tart is baked, the topping should be nicely brown, as should the edges of the pastry, which should also have risen well.

CRUNCHY FRIED POLENTA WITH GOAT'S CHEESE

Serves: 2

This crunchy, golden polenta is made from cornmeal and is a great alternative to everyday carbs such as pasta or potatoes. This recipe uses 'set' polenta, which can be bought in vacuum packs from the supermarket and is quick and easy to fry.

1 tbsp olive oil

1 small red onion, peeled and finely sliced into rings

½ tsp caster sugar

½ tsp thyme, fresh or dried

4 x 1cm-thick slices of ready-made polenta, patted dry using kitchen paper

75g soft goat's cheese, crumbled

Salt and pepper

Salad to serve

* Place 1 teaspoon of the oil into a non-stick frying pan over a medium heat. Add the onion, sugar and thyme, season with salt and pepper and stir well. Cook for around 10–15 minutes until softened. Try not to let the onion brown.

* Meanwhile, warm the remaining oil in a separate frying pan over a medium heat. Add the polenta slices to the pan and fry for around 3 minutes on each side until golden and crunchy.

* Serve the polenta topped with the caramelised onion and goat's cheese, with some salad on the side.

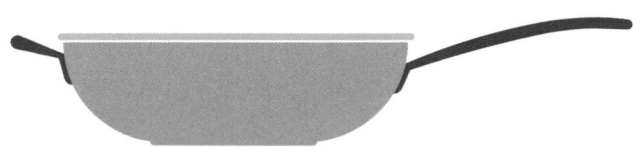

POTATO AND APPLE CAKES

Makes: 4 cakes (serves 2)

These tasty cakes are similar to potato rostï (grated potato cakes).
The apple gives them a nice sweet edge and keeps them moist.
They make a great light meal on their own, or go well served with
vegetarian sausages.

2 medium potatoes
(approx. 400g total weight)

1 very small onion,
peeled and grated

1 small eating apple,
peeled and grated

1 small garlic clove,
peeled and finely chopped

1 tsp fresh herbs, such as
parsley or thyme, chopped

1 medium egg, beaten

1 tbsp olive oil

Salt and pepper

* Place the potatoes in a saucepan of cold water. Bring to the
  boil and cook for 7–9 minutes. Drain well and set aside to cool.

* Once the potatoes are cool, grate them coarsely and place
  into a large bowl with the onion, apple, garlic, herbs and
  egg and season with salt and pepper. Mix well.

* Place the oil in a large non-stick frying pan and warm
  over a medium–hot heat.

* Spoon the mixture into the hot oil in four separate mounds.
  Flatten each mound a little. Cook the cakes for around
  4 minutes on each side until golden and crispy. Serve
  immediately, while hot.

SWEETCORN FRITTERS

Serves: 2

These are like little savoury pancakes, with a soft fluffy texture surrounding juicy corn kernels. They make a cheap and satisfying supper, and go well with this crisp fresh salsa or some salad.

2 large eggs, separated

3 tbsp milk

50g plain flour

½ tsp salt

1 tsp baking powder

200g canned sweetcorn, drained

4–6 tbsp olive oil

For the fresh salsa

6 cherry tomatoes, quartered

3cm piece of cucumber, chopped into 1cm cubes

1 tbsp olive oil

1 tsp chopped fresh herbs, such as parsley or coriander

* To make the fresh salsa, simply mix all the ingredients together in a bowl. Set aside while you make the fritters. (Don't make the salsa too far in advance as it is nicer when freshly mixed.)

* In a large bowl, whisk the egg yolks, milk, flour, salt and baking powder together well. Add the sweetcorn and stir in.

* In a separate bowl, whisk the egg whites until they form stiff peaks. If you have an electric mixer, it is quicker to use it here.

* Gently fold the egg whites into the sweetcorn mixture.

* Heat the olive oil in a large frying pan and drop in tablespoons of the fritter mix.

* Cook for around 1 minute on each side until golden brown. Serve immediately, topped with the fresh salsa.

Tip: To separate an egg, crack it against a bowl and gently pull it apart with your thumbs, keeping the yolk in one side of the shell. Let the white spill into the bowl, then pour the yolk carefully into the other half of the shell, allowing any remaining white to drop out into the bowl. Repeat until all the white is in the bowl.

MEXICAN BEAN CHIMICHANGA

Serves: 1 (Vegan)

A chimichanga is a fried folded tortilla, stuffed full of warm delicious fillings. This one has kidney beans, peppers and lots of fresh flavours. If feeding friends, you can double the quantities here and cook in batches – but keep them warm in the oven while frying the rest.

1 tsp olive oil

1 garlic clove, peeled and finely chopped

100g canned kidney beans, rinsed and drained

½ green pepper, deseeded and cut into 1cm strips

½ red pepper, deseeded and cut into 1cm strips

Pinch of chilli flakes

2 tsp lime juice

2 tsp tomato purée

2 tsp chopped fresh coriander

2 tortilla wraps

100ml sunflower or vegetable oil

Cocktail sticks, for pinning

* Warm the olive oil in a saucepan over a medium heat. Add the garlic and cook for a minute or two until softened.

* Add the beans, peppers, chilli flakes, lime juice and tomato purée and stir together well. Cook gently for around 15 minutes until the beans are heated through, then stir the coriander into the mixture.

* Lay out a tortilla wrap on a board. Heap the filling into the centre. Place another wrap on top and press down around the filling, forming it into a rectangle. Fold up the sides and tuck in the ends, like an envelope. Use several cocktail sticks to pin the chimichanga together.

* Pour the oil into a frying pan, so that it is around 1cm deep. Heat over a high temperature. When the oil is hot, drop in a tiny piece of tortilla. It should sizzle but not brown. If it doesn't sizzle, let the oil heat for a minute or two more. If the tortilla piece browns quickly, turn the heat down.

* Place the chimichanga into the hot oil, seam-side down. Cook for a minute or two until browned. Carefully turn over and cook the other side. You can pull out the cocktail sticks or rearrange if necessary.

* Finally, prop the chimichanga up on each side to make sure that all four sides are cooked. Remove from the oil and place on some kitchen paper to blot the excess oil. Take out the cocktail sticks, cut in half and serve immediately!

POTATO AND THYME QUESADILLA

Serves: 1–2

A quesadilla is like a Mexican version of a toastie! They're quick and easy to rustle up and great for feeding friends as they can be made in large quantities and always please a crowd. Vary the fillings and toppings however you fancy – see page 136 for another suggestion.

1 tsp olive oil

100g waxy salad potatoes, cut into 1cm chunks

½ garlic clove, peeled and finely chopped

½ tsp thyme, fresh or dried

2 tortilla wraps

75g mature Cheddar cheese, grated

Salt and pepper

* Heat the oil in a small saucepan over a high heat. Add the potato chunks and cook for around 15–20 minutes until browned and tender. Add the garlic and cook for a minute or two until fragrant. Add the thyme, season with salt and pepper and stir well.

* Lay a tortilla wrap on a board. Spoon the potato mixture onto it and sprinkle over the cheese, up to 2cm from the edge.

* Place the second tortilla on top of the mixture and press down to form a kind of tortilla sandwich.

* Warm a large non-stick frying pan over a medium–hot heat. Note that you don't need to use oil to cook the quesadillas.

* Transfer the filled tortillas into the dry frying pan. After about 1½ minutes, you should notice the tortilla browning. Flip it over and cook the other side.

* The quesadilla is ready to serve when the cheese is melted inside and the tortillas are both browned.

* Cut up the quesadilla into quarters and serve immediately.

BLACK BEAN AND AVOCADO QUESADILLA

Serves: 1–2

Here's another quesadilla recipe that your friends will love (or see page 135 for a hearty potato version). Made using shop-bought tortilla wraps, these are great as a quick supper, or can be cut into triangles and shared around as snacks.

200g canned black beans, drained and rinsed

1 spring onion, finely sliced

40g mature Cheddar cheese, grated

¼ tsp ground cumin

¼ tsp ground oregano

Finely grated zest and juice of ½ lime

1 small, ripe avocado

2 large tortilla wraps

Chilli powder, to sprinkle (optional)

* Place the black beans, sliced spring onion, grated cheese, cumin, oregano and lime zest into a bowl and lightly mash together using a fork or potato masher. You don't want it to be a purée, just crush the beans slightly and mix the ingredients together.

* Remove the skin and stone from the avocado, slice the flesh into 1cm thick strips and pour the lime juice over the top. Stir gently to coat the slices of avocado in lime juice.

* Lay a tortilla wrap on a board. Spoon the bean mixture onto the tortilla and, using the back of a spoon, spread the mixture evenly over the tortilla, up to 2cm from the edge.

* Place the second tortilla on top of the bean mixture and press down to form a kind of tortilla sandwich.

* Warm a large non-stick frying pan over a medium–hot heat. Note that you don't need to use oil to cook the quesadillas.

* Transfer the filled tortillas into the dry frying pan. After about 1½ minutes, you will notice the tortilla browning. At this point, flip it over to cook the other side.

* The quesadilla is ready to serve when the cheese inside is melted and the tortillas are both browned.

* Cut up the quesadilla into quarters and place on a plate. Drain the avocado slices from the lime juice and place them on top of the quesadillas or on the side. Dust with chilli powder, if using, and serve immediately.

FEEDING FRIENDS

BEANY NACHOS

Serves: 6–8

Nachos are the perfect food to enjoy with friends. They disappear in minutes at parties or when watching a film, and are good as a starter or even when you are nursing a hangover! If you feel like pushing the boat out, load these high with soured cream, guacamole and red onion too.

1 tbsp olive oil

1 garlic clove, peeled and finely chopped

1 onion, peeled and finely chopped

2 x 400g cans kidney beans in chilli sauce

2 x 400g cans chopped tomatoes

1 large packet of plain tortilla chips (no need to buy expensive ones here)

100g cheese (Cheddar, Monterey Jack or similar), grated

Add extras to your taste

Tomato salsa

Guacamole

Soured cream

Sliced red onion

* Preheat the grill to its highest setting.

* Warm the oil in a non-stick frying pan over a low–medium heat. Add the garlic and onion and cook for around 5 minutes until the onion and garlic soften and brown very lightly.

* Add the beans (including their sauce) and the tomatoes and cook for around 20 minutes until the sauce has thickened. Stir occasionally.

* Spread the tortilla chips evenly over the base of a large baking dish and pour the bean and tomato mixture over the top. Sprinkle with cheese and put the dish under the grill for around 3–4 minutes until the cheese is well melted.

* Serve the beany nachos as they are, or add salsa, guacamole, soured cream or sliced red onion if you fancy.

HONEY-BAKED VEGETABLE CRISPS

Serves: 4

Homemade crisps are much healthier than shop-bought bags and you can be as inventive as you like with the ingredients. Parsnips are particularly delicious. These are best eaten while fresh.

4 x root vegetables of your choice (such as parsnip, carrot, sweet potato or beetroot)

2 tsp runny honey

Salt and pepper

Large baking sheet

Non-stick baking paper

* Preheat the oven to 180°C Fan/Gas Mark 6. Line a large baking sheet with non-stick baking paper.

* Peel the skin off the vegetables, then peel the actual vegetables into fat strips using a potato peeler. Lay the strips on the baking sheet, not overlapping.

* Drizzle the honey evenly over the chips and season with salt and pepper. Bake for 10–15 minutes until crisp, but not brown. Eat while still warm from the oven.

BAKED CAMEMBERT

Serves: 4–6

This is like instant cheese fondu! Serve it directly to the table and let everyone dip their bread or vegetables into the gooey melted cheese.

1 Camembert cheese

1 garlic clove, peeled and finely sliced

½ tsp dried or a couple of sprigs of fresh thyme or rosemary

1 tsp olive oil

Bread, celery and carrot sticks, to serve

* Preheat the oven to 200°C Fan/Gas Mark 7.

* Take the Camembert out of the plastic packaging. If there are any stickers on the cheese, remove these too. Place the cheese back into the wooden box base.

* Lay the slices of garlic over the cheese. Sprinkle with the thyme or rosemary. If you are using fresh herbs, just lay the sprigs on top.

* Drizzle with the olive oil and place the lid back onto the box. Place the cheese onto a baking tray and bake in the oven for 15 minutes.

* Carefully remove the cheese from the oven and place the hot cheese, still in the box, on a plate. Remove the lid and serve with fresh bread and celery or carrot sticks.

VEGGIE TOAD IN THE HOLE WITH ONION GRAVY

Serves: 2

Great as an alternative Sunday lunch, toad in the hole is such a crowd-pleaser and works perfectly with vegetarian sausages. It's a cheap meal to put together, although you might want to add extra sausages if you're feeding big appetites.

For the toad in the hole
150ml full-fat milk

1 large egg

65g plain flour

3 tbsp sunflower oil

4 vegetarian sausages

Salt and pepper

For the onion gravy
1 tsp sunflower oil

1 medium onion, peeled and chopped into thin slices

1 tsp plain flour

1 tsp sugar

300ml vegetable stock

1 tsp Worcestershire sauce (if you eat fish) or Henderson's Relish (if you don't)

Salt and pepper

* Preheat the oven to 200°C Fan/Gas Mark 7.

* Pour the milk into a jug, crack in the egg and whisk well.

* Sift the flour through a sieve into a bowl and season with salt and pepper. Pour in the milk and egg mixture.

* Whisk well until the batter is smooth and the flour is incorporated. Leave the batter to rest for 30 minutes before using.

* Pour the oil into a large non-stick roasting tin and place in the oven for 3–4 minutes to heat up.

* Add the sausages and bake for 15 minutes until they just start to brown, then remove the tin from the oven. Quickly, so the oil stays really hot, pour the batter into the tin around the sausages and put them back in the oven. Bake for 25–30 minutes until golden, well risen and crisp.

* Meanwhile, make the onion gravy. Heat the oil in a frying pan, add the onion and cook for 5 minutes until it starts to soften.

* Add the flour and sugar and stir to coat the onion. Add the stock and Worcestershire or Henderson's sauce and season with salt and pepper. Leave to bubble away gently until the toad in the hole is ready to serve.

* Serve the toad in the hole immediately with the onion gravy on the side.

Tip: Make sure the oil is really hot when pouring the batter into the tin. This will help it to rise.

MEDITERRANEAN VEGETABLE CALZONE

Serves: 1–2

A calzone is a pizza that has been folded in half and sealed. It's a bit like a jumbo Cornish pasty, but made with dough instead of pastry. If you can't be bothered to roast the vegetables from scratch, you can buy bags of frozen chargrilled vegetables from larger supermarkets. Simply multiply the recipe if you're feeding more mouths.

For the dough

200g strong white bread, plus extra for dusting

⅓ tsp fast-action dried yeast

¼ tsp sugar

125ml warm water

2 tsp olive oil

For the filling

3 tbsp tomato purée or homemade tomato sauce (page 18)

3–4 tbsp roasted vegetables (see page 129)

70g mozzarella cheese torn into pieces

Large baking sheet

* Sift the flour and salt through a sieve into a large mixing bowl and add the yeast and sugar. Add the warm water (it should be body temperature) and 1 teaspoon of the oil and mix until the ingredients come together into a sticky dough.

* Turn out the dough onto a floured work surface and knead gently for a couple of minutes until the dough starts to feel smoother.

* Place the dough back into the bowl, cover with cling film and a clean tea towel and leave in a warm place to rise for an hour. This can be near a warm oven or in the sunlight by a window. The dough should almost double in size.

* Preheat the oven to 220°C Fan/Gas Mark 9. Grease a large baking sheet lightly with the remaining 1 teaspoon of oil.

* Turn out the dough onto a lightly floured surface again and knead gently for around 5 minutes until it feels smooth, elastic and less sticky. Shape the dough into a circle as thick or thin as you like.

* Transfer the dough to the baking sheet and cover with tomato purée or sauce, leaving a 3cm margin around the edge of the dough. Place the vegetables and cheese in the middle.

* Dip your finger into a cup of cold water and dab it lightly all around the edge of the calzone. Fold it in half to form a half moon shape. Crimp the edges to seal the calzone.

* Bake for 15 minutes, then slide the calzone off the baking sheet onto the oven shelf and bake for another 2–3 minutes until golden and crispy.

* Serve immediately. Any leftovers are great cold for a packed lunch the next day.

LENTIL MOUSSAKA

Serves: 4–6

Moussaka is a Greek dish that's sort of like lasagne, but with layers of aubergine instead of pasta. This vegetarian version replaces mince with lentils, which make it filling and hearty. Cooked puy lentils can be bought in cans or pouches and are much quicker and easier to use than dried ones.

For the aubergine filling

2 tbsp olive oil

1 medium onion, peeled and chopped

2 garlic cloves, peeled and chopped

2 aubergines, cut into 1cm cubes

100g cooked puy lentils, from a pouch or can, drained

1 tsp ground cinnamon

1 tsp ground oregano

400g can chopped tomatoes

2 tbsp tomato purée

Salt and pepper

For the topping

300g full-fat natural yoghurt

60g plain flour

2 large egg yolks (see Tip on page 132 for separating eggs)

120g mature Cheddar cheese, finely grated

* Preheat the oven to 180°C Fan/Gas Mark 6.

* Heat the oil in a large frying pan over a medium heat. Add the onion and cook for 5 minutes or so until it starts to soften. Add the garlic and cook for another 2 minutes or so.

* Add the cubes of aubergine and cook for 10–15 minutes until they soften and start to shrink. Then, add the lentils, cinnamon, oregano, tomatoes, tomato purée and seasoning. Leave to bubble away gently.

* Meanwhile, start on the topping. Place the yoghurt, flour and egg yolks together in a bowl and whisk. Set aside.

* In a large baking dish, spread out the aubergine and tomato mixture right to the edges and smooth it over with the back of a spoon. Cover evenly with the topping.

* Sprinkle the Cheddar cheese over the top.

* Bake for 30–40 minutes until the topping is golden and bubbling.

BLUE CHEESE AND LEEK FILO TARTS

Serves: 6

These gorgeous little tarts are full of flavour and bound to impress your friends at dinner parties. Serve with a fresh green salad.

30g butter

2 leeks, washed and thinly sliced

3 sheets of filo pastry

3 large eggs

100g vegetarian blue cheese, such as Dolcelatte or Stilton

100ml double cream

Salt and pepper

Muffin tray

Tip: Save little foil pie trays or free ceramic dishes or ramekins to use here if you don't have a muffin tray.

* Place about a third of the butter in a saucepan and melt over a medium heat. Add the leeks and allow them to soften gently, but not colour, for at least 15 minutes, stirring regularly.

* Preheat the oven to 200°C Fan/Gas Mark 7.

* Fold a sheet of filo pastry in half lengthways, then in half again, so you have a rectangle that is four layers thick. Cut the rectangle in half to make two squares. Set aside, covered with a clean tea towel. Repeat with the remaining pastry sheets so that you have six squares. Set aside, again covered.

* Melt the rest of the butter in a small saucepan over a low heat, then grease six holes of a muffin tray lightly with some of the melted butter. Lay a filo square in each hole of the muffin tray. These will be your tart cases. Press the pastry into the sides of the holes and brush each one with more melted butter.

* Once all six pastry cases are brushed with melted butter, bake for 5 minutes in the oven.

* Meanwhile, place the eggs into a large bowl and whisk well. Crumble in the blue cheese. Pour in the cream, season with salt and pepper and tip in the softened leeks. Whisk together gently so the ingredients are well combined.

* Once the pastry cases have been baked, remove from the oven. Spoon the egg mixture evenly into the cases. Fill until they are level with the top of the tray, no more, else the mixture will spill out.

* Bake the tarts for a further 12–15 minutes until the pastry is golden and the filling is set.

BEETROOT TART

Serves: 4–6

This impressive tart is much easier to make than it looks and will become a talking point at any dinner party! Be very careful when turning it out of the tin, as beetroot can stain clothes and work surfaces. Do it over the sink to be on the safe side!

30g butter, plus extra for greasing

250g cooked beetroot in natural juices (approx. 4 beetroot), cut into 1cm thick slices

1 heaped tsp thyme, fresh or frozen

2 tsp honey

250g ready-rolled puff pastry, fridge-cold

Salt and pepper

20cm round springform cake tin

Large baking sheet

* Preheat the oven to 180°C Fan/Gas Mark 6. Grease a 20cm round springform cake tin with butter.

* Melt the butter in a large frying pan over a medium heat. Add the beetroot slices, sprinkle over the thyme and honey, and season with salt and pepper. Cook the beetroot slices for around 5 minutes on each side.

* Arrange the beetroot slices in the bottom of the cake tin and pour the buttery sauce over the top.

* Lay out your puff pastry and cut out a circle about 1cm larger than the tin. Place the pastry over the beetroot and tuck the excess pastry down around the edge of the tin. Prick the pastry a couple of times on top using a sharp knife.

* Place the cake tin on a baking sheet and bake the tart in the oven for 25–30 minutes until the pastry is golden brown.

* Remove from the oven and leave the tart to rest for 5 minutes in the tin before removing the sides of the tin (you may wish to run a knife around the edge first).

* Place a plate over the tart, hold them together tightly and flip over, to turn the tart out onto the plate. This is best done over the sink, in case it goes wrong or any liquid escapes, as beetroot stains everything it touches!

* Remove the base of the cake tin and serve immediately, ideally with salad.

LEMON COURGETTE TART

Serves: 4

This pretty tart may look fancy but in fact is very easy to create – the secret is ready-rolled pastry, which means all the hard work has been done for you. With fresh flavours and flaky pastry, it's good served hot with salad. Or allow to cool, then wrap slices in foil for a packed lunch.

2 large courgettes, sliced lengthways into 5mm thick slices

1 tbsp olive oil

375g packet of ready-rolled puff pastry, fridge-cold

1 tbsp basil pesto

1 tbsp milk

3 garlic cloves, peeled and thinly sliced

Zest of 1 unwaxed lemon, sliced into thin strips

50g vegetarian Parmesan cheese, finely grated

1 tsp lemon juice

Large baking sheet
Non-stick baking paper

* Preheat the oven to 180°C Fan/Gas Mark 6 and line a large baking sheet with non-stick baking paper.

* Place the slices of courgette in a roasting tin and drizzle the olive oil evenly over them. Place in the oven and bake for 6 minutes.

* Unroll the puff pastry onto the prepared baking sheet. If it does not fit, just halve it and make two tarts on two sheets.

* Use a sharp knife to score a border within the pastry rectangle, scoring parallel to the edge of the pastry but roughly 2–3cm in from it.

* Spread the pesto inside the inner rectangle you have just marked out. Brush the milk around the outer border of the pastry, either using a pastry brush, or just dabbing it on with your fingers.

* When the courgettes have been baked for 6 minutes, remove the tin from the oven and place the slices of garlic and lemon zest on the slices of courgette. Return to the oven for a further 6 minutes.

* When the courgettes have been baked a second time, remove them from the oven and discard the garlic and lemon zest. Arrange the slices of courgette on the pesto-covered area of the pastry.

* Sprinkle the Parmesan evenly over the slices of courgette and bake for 18–20 minutes.

* When the tart is baked, the topping should be nicely brown, as should the edges of the pastry, which should also have risen well.

* Gently drizzle the lemon juice sparingly over the courgettes and serve the tart while hot.

SPICED SWEET POTATO AND SQUASH TART

Serves: 4

This colourful tart looks totally gorgeous with its assortment of red and orange ingredients! Yet it's very simple to make, with shop-bought pastry and no need for a tart tin. The potatoes and squash mean it's filling enough to have for dinner with just a bit of salad on the side.

1 small sweet potato, peeled and cut into 1cm cubes

200g butternut squash, peeled, deseeded and cut into 1cm cubes

1 red onion, peeled and cut into chunks

8 cherry tomatoes

1 tbsp olive oil

1 tsp ground cumin

1 tsp ground cinnamon

½ tsp chilli powder

275g ready-rolled puff pastry, fridge-cold

Splash of milk

100g feta cheese, crumbled

Salt and pepper

Large baking sheet
Non-stick baking paper

* Preheat the oven to 180°C Fan/Gas Mark 6 and line a large baking sheet with non-stick baking paper.

* Place the sweet potato, squash, onion, tomatoes, oil, cumin, cinnamon and chilli together into a bowl, season with salt and pepper and toss together. Spread the vegetables out in a roasting tin and bake for 10 minutes until softened.

* Meanwhile, unroll the puff pastry onto the prepared baking sheet. If it doesn't fit, just halve it and make two tarts on two sheets.

* Use a sharp knife to score a border within the pastry rectangle, scoring parallel to the edge of the pastry but roughly 2–3cm in from it.

* Once the vegetables have been baked, transfer them to the pastry sheet, laying them out evenly within the inner rectangle. Brush the milk around the outer border of the pastry, either using a pastry brush, or just dabbing it on with your fingers.

* Sprinkle the feta evenly over the vegetables and bake for 18–20 minutes.

* When the tart is baked, the topping should be nicely brown, as should the edges of the pastry, which should also have risen well. Serve the tart while hot.

BUTTERNUT SQUASH AND TOMATO GRATIN

Serves: 4

A gratin is a hearty oven-baked dish of vegetables or potatoes baked in a creamy sauce with a crisp, crunchy topping. This butternut squash version has a herby, cheesy crust and is very easy to make. It can be eaten for dinner or served as a side with another dish.

1 large butternut squash, peeled, deseeded and cut into 1cm thick slices

1 tbsp olive oil

400g can chopped tomatoes

150ml double cream

60g vegetarian Parmesan cheese, finely grated

½ tsp rosemary, fresh or dried

½ tsp thyme, fresh or dried

Salt and pepper

* Preheat the oven to 200°C Fan/Gas Mark 7.

* Take a large roasting tin and lay out the slices of squash flat in the tin. Drizzle the oil evenly over the slices.

* Bake for around 25 minutes in the oven until they are tender.

* Once the squash has been baked, transfer the slices to a baking dish.

* Pour over the can of tomatoes, evenly covering the squash, and do the same with the cream.

* Evenly sprinkle the Parmesan, rosemary and thyme over the top of the gratin, and season with salt and pepper.

* Return to the oven and bake for a further 20 minutes until golden and bubbling.

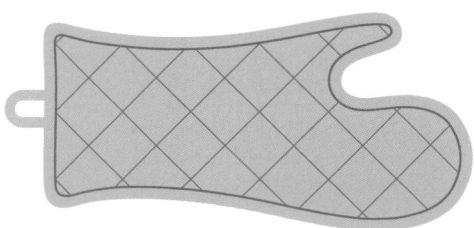

CHEDDAR AND LEEK QUICHE

Serves: 6

Far more delicious than a shop-bought quiche, this has lovely crunchy poppy-seed pastry, but if pushed for time you can use ready-made shortcrust pastry instead. The cold quiche can be cut into wedges and kept in the fridge for 2–3 days.

For the pastry

140g wholemeal flour

¼ tsp salt

1 tbsp poppy seeds

65g butter, cold and cubed

65ml cold water

For the quiche

10g butter

2 large leeks, washed and cut into 1cm thick rings

3 large eggs

200ml double cream

150ml milk

150g mature Cheddar or strong hard cheese, grated

20cm round springform cake tin, or fluted tart tin

Non-stick baking paper

Tip: Baking beans are used to weigh down pastry while baking, so that it stays flat. If you don't have any, simply use 500g dried lentils/beans.

* Preheat the oven to 180°C Fan/Gas Mark 6. Grease a 20cm round springform cake tin (or fluted tart tin if you have one).

* Sift the flour and salt through a sieve into a mixing bowl, then stir in the poppy seeds. Add the butter and rub into the flour with your fingertips until the mixture looks like breadcrumbs.

* Pour in the water and mix until the dough comes together. It should feel slightly sticky to the touch, but not enough to stick to your hands. If it won't come together, add a tiny bit more water – literally just a few drops – and mix again. Wrap the pastry ball in cling film and chill for 20 minutes to firm up.

* When the pastry has chilled, unwrap and place between two large sheets of cling film. Roll out between the sheets until big enough to fit the tin and around 5mm in thickness.

* Fit the pastry into the tin and press gently into the sides. Prick all over with a fork and line with non-stick baking paper. Fill the case with baking beans (see Tip), right to the edges. Bake for 15 minutes until crisp and starting to brown in places. Remove the beans and baking paper and set aside to cool.

* Melt the butter in a non-stick frying pan over a medium heat. Add the leeks and cook for 10–15 minutes until soft, but not brown.

* In a bowl, whisk together the eggs, cream, milk and half the cheese. Stir in the leek. Pour this mixture into the cooled pastry case and sprinkle the remaining cheese on top.

* Bake the quiche for 15 minutes, then turn the temperature down to 160°C Fan/Gas Mark 4 and cook for 30 minutes more. The filling will become golden brown and firm once cooked. The egg mixture may puff up, but will drop back down once cool.

SPICED VEGETABLE PARCELS

Makes: 4

These easy parcels do call for quite a few spices but they are all everyday ones that are useful to keep in your cupboard for a whole range of recipes. Honey and apricots add a nice sweetness to the mixture. The parcels are lovely served with couscous or the bulghur wheat on page 88. Any leftovers are great in a packed lunch.

100g fresh or frozen spinach

1 tbsp olive oil

1 medium onion, peeled and chopped

1 medium butternut squash (approx. 750g), deseeded, peeled and cut into 1cm cubes

1 tsp each of ground cumin, coriander and paprika

Generous pinch of chilli powder

100g canned chickpeas, drained and rinsed

8 dried apricots, chopped

2 tsp honey

3 tbsp tomato purée

2 tsp chopped fresh herbs, e.g. coriander, mint or parsley (optional)

375g packet of ready-rolled puff pastry, fridge-cold

Flour, for dusting work surface

1 large egg, beaten

2 tbsp sesame seeds (optional)

Large baking sheet

Non-stick baking paper

* If using frozen spinach, defrost fully before you begin, and press in a sieve to remove all excess water.

* Warm the oil in a large frying pan over a medium heat. Add the onion and butternut squash and cook gently for around 10 minutes until the onion is softened (but don't let it brown).

* Add the cumin, coriander, paprika and chilli, and stir well. Add the chickpeas, apricots, honey and tomato purée and mix to ensure everything is well combined. Stir in the spinach and herbs, if you are using them, and turn off the heat. Allow the mixture to cool a little.

* Preheat the oven to 200°C Fan/Gas Mark 7 and line a large baking sheet with non-stick baking paper.

* Unroll the sheet of pastry on a lightly floured work surface. Cut the pastry into four rectangles.

* Place a couple of spoonfuls of the vegetable mixture into the centre of each pastry rectangle. Fold up the two long sides of pastry over the filling and squeeze together at the top to seal. Fold up the shorter sides and squeeze them together, too, to create a little parcel.

* Place the parcels (seam facing down) onto the prepared baking sheet and brush them well with beaten egg. If you are using sesame seeds, sprinkle them over the parcels now.

* Bake for 20–25 minutes until the parcels are golden and crisp.

TEMPURA VEGETABLES WITH SOY DIPPING SAUCE

Serves: 4 (Vegan)

Tempura is a very light, crisp batter, which is used to coat vegetables for frying. These are perfect for nibbles or as a starter for a dinner party, served with this delicious zingy dipping sauce.

For the vegetables

50g cornflour

75g plain flour

150ml sparkling water

250ml sunflower
or vegetable oil

400g vegetables of your choice, chopped and sliced into small pieces (try peppers, broccoli, aubergine and courgettes)

For the soy dipping sauce

1 tbsp soy sauce

1 tbsp lime juice

1 tsp sugar

1 tbsp sweet chilli sauce

* Start by preparing the batter. Sift the flours through a sieve into a mixing bowl. Add the water and whisk together to form a smooth batter that will stick to your finger when you dip it into the mixture.

* Now, make the dipping sauce. Place all the ingredients together into a bowl and whisk together. Set aside.

* Heat the oil in a large sturdy saucepan over a high heat. Make sure you do not leave the pan unattended.

* When the oil is hot, dip the vegetable pieces into the batter and make sure they are well covered. Then carefully drop them into the oil, a couple at a time, and cook for just a minute or so until the batter is puffy and lightly browned. Remove from the oil using a slotted spoon and place on a plate covered in kitchen paper to drain.

* Once all the vegetables are cooked, make sure you turn off the heat under the pan and allow the oil to cool. Leave the vegetables to cool for 5 minutes as they will be really hot, then dive in, dipping them into the sauce while still warm.

ROASTED VEGETABLE ENCHILADAS

Serves: 4

Enchiladas are tortilla wraps stuffed with gorgeous fillings and baked until hot and bubbling. These ones are filled with feta, roasted veggies and a rich tomato sauce, and smothered in melted cheese. Yum!

For the vegetables

3 peppers (any colour you like, but a mixture is good), deseeded and cut into 2cm chunks

1 red onion, peeled and cut into eighths

2 courgettes, sliced into 1cm thick rings

1 tbsp olive oil

For the tomato sauce

2 tsp olive oil

2 garlic cloves, peeled and chopped

400g can chopped tomatoes

1 tsp caster sugar

1 tsp ground cinnamon

Salt and pepper

To assemble the enchiladas

4 large tortilla wraps

100g fresh spinach leaves

150g feta cheese, crumbled

100g mature Cheddar or Monterey Jack cheese, grated

* Preheat the oven to 180°C Fan/Gas Mark 6.

* Lay out the vegetables in a large roasting tin. Drizzle with olive oil and bake for 20 minutes until tender. Remove from the oven once cooked.

* For the tomato sauce, warm the olive oil in a small saucepan over a medium heat. Add the garlic and cook for 2 minutes until fragrant.

* Add the chopped tomatoes, sugar and cinnamon, then season with salt and pepper. Allow to cook for around 15 minutes until the sauce has thickened.

* Once the vegetables are roasted and the sauce is prepared, you can assemble the enchiladas.

* Lay a tortilla wrap on a board. Spread a quarter of the tomato sauce evenly on the wrap. Lay some spinach leaves on top. Top with roasted vegetables and feta cheese and roll up, but don't tuck in the ends. Place the enchilada into a baking dish, seam-side down. Repeat to create four enchiladas.

* Sprinkle with the grated cheese and bake for 20–30 minutes until the filling is bubbling and the cheese is golden and melted. Serve immediately.

IN BREAD AND ON TOAST

FIVE-MINUTE WHOLEMEAL BREAD

Makes: 1 loaf

If you've ever wondered why you might want to make your own bread when it's so much easier to buy it, give this recipe a go, and you'll soon understand. With no complicated kneading or rising, this recipe takes just 5 minutes from cupboard to oven, then you simply leave it to bake. Fresh, warm, homemade bread for minimal effort!

Sunflower or vegetable oil, for greasing

400ml milk

1 tbsp lemon juice

300g wholemeal flour

300g plain flour, plus extra for dusting the work surface

1 tsp salt

1 tsp bicarbonate of soda

40g melted butter

1 tbsp treacle

900g loaf tin

* Preheat the oven to 210°C Fan/Gas Mark 8. Grease a 900g loaf tin all over with oil.

* Combine the milk and lemon juice in a jug and stir gently. Set aside.

* Sift both types of flour, the salt and bicarbonate of soda through a sieve into a large mixing bowl. Use your hands to make a well (hole) in the centre of the mixture.

* Pour the milk mixture, melted butter and treacle into the well in the centre of the flour mixture and gradually mix until all the flour is combined. It will be a wet and slightly sticky dough.

* Generously dust your work surface with flour (make sure it is clean and dry first!) and turn the dough out onto the floured surface. Knead gently with your fists for just a minute until the dough forms a smooth ball.

* Place the dough in the tin, sprinkle with flour, and bake for 40–45 minutes until the loaf is golden brown on top. To check it is cooked, turn it out of the tin (wearing oven gloves as it will be very hot!) and tap it on the bottom. If done, it will sound hollow. If not, place back in the tin and return to the oven for a further 5 minutes, then test again.

* Once cooked, remove the loaf immediately from the tin and place on a wire rack to cool for at least 30 minutes before slicing it up.

* Store in an airtight container and eat within 2–3 days. Once cool, the bread can be frozen in a sealed freezer bag for up to 3 months. If you want to toast from frozen, remember to slice it first.

BRIE AND CRANBERRY PANINI

Serves: 1

Why give your cash to the local cafe when you can make a delicious warm panini at home? This one is full of gooey melted brie, and the dollop of cranberry sauce really jazzes up a simple sarnie.

1 panini roll
1–2 tsp cranberry sauce
3–4 slices of Brie

* Preheat the grill to high.

* Cut the panini roll in half lengthways. Toast the outside of the halves lightly until warm. Turn both pieces over and toast the insides. This will help keep the filling hot.

* Spread the cranberry sauce inside the roll. Lay the slices of Brie on top.

* Close the roll, press down and grill for 3–4 minutes until the cheese is melted. Cut in half and eat straight away.

MOZZARELLA, TOMATO AND BASIL PANINI

Serves: 1

Could your sandwich be any more Italian? These flavours were made to go together and the mozzarella becomes lovely and stringy when warm.

1 panini roll
1–2 tsp basil pesto
50g mozzarella cheese, sliced
2–3 slices of tomato
Couple of fresh basil leaves

* Preheat the grill to high

* Cut the panini roll in half lengthways. Toast the outside of the halves lightly until warm, then turn both pieces over and toast the insides. This will help keep the filling hot.

* Spread the pesto inside the roll. Fill with mozzarella, tomato and basil.

* Close the roll, press down and grill for 3–4 minutes until the cheese is melted and bubbling. Cut in half and eat straight away.

HOUMOUS, SPINACH AND TOMATO PANINI

Serves: 1 (Vegan)

A simple but wholesome filling to see you through the afternoon. Don't forget to add salt and pepper to bring out the flavours.

1 panini roll

50g houmous

Small handful of fresh baby spinach leaves

2–3 slices of tomato

Salt and pepper

* Preheat the grill to high.

* Cut the panini roll in half lengthways. Toast the outside of the halves lightly until warm, then turn both pieces over and toast the insides. This will help keep the filling hot.

* Spread the houmous inside the roll. Season with salt and pepper.

* Fill the roll with the spinach leaves and tomato slices.

* Close the roll, press down and grill for 3–4 minutes until the filling is warmed through. Cut in half and eat straight away.

BLUE CHEESE, OLIVE AND PEPPER PANINI

Serves: 1

If you love strong flavours, this is the sandwich for you! Remember that not all blue cheese is suitable for vegetarians, so check the label. Fresh olives are nicest if you feel like splashing out, otherwise buy a jar or can.

1 panini roll

35g vegetarian blue cheese, such as Dolcelatte

4 olives, pitted and cut in half

¼ pepper, colour of choice, deseeded and thinly sliced

* Preheat the grill to high.

* Cut the panini roll in half lengthways. Toast the outside of the halves lightly until warm, then turn both pieces over and toast the insides. This will help keep the filling hot.

* Spread the cheese inside the roll. Lay the olives and pepper slices on top.

* Close the roll, press down and grill for 3–4 minutes until the cheese is warmed through. Cut in half and eat straight away.

GARLIC MUSHROOMS ON TOAST

Serves: 1

These buttery, garlicky mushrooms make a brilliant lunch or quick supper. Try using large, flat mushrooms, such as portobello, which have a lovely flavour.

15g butter

1 garlic clove,
peeled and crushed

100g mushrooms, thinly sliced

½ tsp dried thyme

2 slices of ciabatta bread
or baguette

Salt and pepper

* Melt the butter in a saucepan over a medium heat. Add the garlic and cook for a minute or two until fragrant.

* Add the mushrooms. Stir to ensure they become well coated in melted butter.

* Add the thyme, season with salt and pepper and cook for around 15 minutes. Make sure any water from the mushrooms is cooked off.

* Toast the bread and top with the cooked mushrooms. Enjoy immediately!

GOAT'S CHEESE AND HONEY ON TOAST

Serves: 1

This sweet, creamy topping turns a simple slice of toast into a real treat.

2 slices of ciabatta bread or baguette

30g soft goat's cheese

Drizzle of honey

* Toast the slices of bread on both sides.

* Spread the goat's cheese onto the toast. Drizzle with the honey and enjoy immediately.

FETA, TOMATOES AND OLIVES ON TOAST

Serves: 1

This Mediterranean mixture packs a punch in the flavour department and is also a rather healthy lunch option.

40g feta cheese, crumbled

6 cherry tomatoes, halved

4 black olives, pitted and chopped in half

2 tsp olive oil

2 slices of ciabatta bread or baguette

* Place the feta, tomatoes, olives and oil into a bowl and mix well.

* Toast the slices of bread on both sides.

* Spoon the topping onto the toast and enjoy immediately.

CHEESE AND LEEK RAREBIT

Serves: 1–2

A perfect late-night snack, rarebit is the ultimate cheese on toast. Leeks are a nice way to add some extra flavour.

½ tsp butter

¼ leek, washed and thinly sliced

2 large, thick slices of bread

1 medium egg

90g Cheddar cheese, grated

Salt and pepper

* Melt the butter in a small frying pan over a medium heat. Add the leek and cook for around 10 minutes until it's really nice and soft. Be careful not to let it brown.

* Meanwhile, preheat the grill, place the bread on the grill tray and toast on both sides.

* Crack the egg into a bowl. Add the grated cheese, salt and pepper and whisk together well.

* When the leek is cooked, place it in the bowl with the egg and cheese and stir in.

* Top the toasted bread on the grill tray with this mixture and place back under the hot grill for 2–3 minutes until the topping is bubbling and golden brown.

* Enjoy immediately, while hot.

BLUE CHEESE RAREBIT

Serves: 1–2

A creamy hit of flavour, perfect for those who enjoy strong cheese.
Remember that not all blue cheese is suitable for vegetarians,
so make sure you check the label.

2 large, thick slices of bread

50g vegetarian blue cheese, such as Stilton or Dolcelatte, crumbled or broken into small pieces

35ml double cream

Pepper

* Preheat the grill, place the bread on the grill tray and toast on both sides.

* Place your cheese, cream and pepper into a bowl. Whisk together to break up the cheese as much as you can.

* Top the toasted bread on the grill tray with this mixture. It will be a little runny.

* Place the toast back under the hot grill and toast for 2–3 minutes until the topping is bubbling and golden brown.

* Enjoy immediately, while hot.

CHEESE AND BEER RAREBIT

Serves: 1

Beer and cheese are a great partnership, especially when melted
together on toast!

2 large, thick slices of bread

1 medium egg

90g Cheddar cheese, grated

1 tbsp strong good-quality beer or stout

Salt and pepper

* Preheat the grill, place the bread on the grill tray and toast on both sides.

* Crack the egg into a bowl. Add the grated cheese, beer, salt and pepper and whisk together well.

* Top the toasted bread on the grill tray with this mixture and place back under the hot grill for 2–3 minutes until the topping is bubbling and golden brown.

* Enjoy immediately, while hot.

GARLIC BUTTER BRUSCHETTA

Serves: 1

You can't go wrong with warm garlic toast! This quick, tasty treat is the perfect nibble to have with drinks.

25g butter

1 garlic clove,
peeled and crushed

2 slices of ciabatta bread
or baguette

* Melt the butter in a small frying pan over a medium heat. Add the garlic and cook for a minute or two until fragrant.

* Toast the slices of bread.

* Drizzle the garlic butter over the bread and dive in immediately.

WHITE BEAN BRUSCHETTA

Serves: 1 (Vegan)

This warm, buttery, garlicky snack takes beans on toast to a whole new level!

25g butter

1 garlic clove,
peeled and crushed

2 tbsp canned cannellini
or butter beans, drained
and rinsed

2 slices of ciabatta bread
or baguette

Drizzle of olive oil

Salt and pepper

* Melt the butter in a small frying pan over a medium heat. Add the garlic and cook for a minute or two until fragrant. Add the beans and cook for 5 minutes or so until they are heated through. Season with salt and pepper.

* Toast the slices of bread.

* Spoon the beans over the bread, drizzle with olive oil and dive in immediately.

TOMATO BRUSCHETTA

Serves: 1 (Vegan)

A classic Italian starter of juicy tomatoes on garlic toast. Great for a simple lunch, supper or snack.

4 cherry tomatoes

2 tsp olive oil

2 slices of ciabatta bread or baguette

1 small garlic clove, peeled

Few fresh basil leaves (optional)

Salt and pepper

* Chop up the cherry tomatoes into small pieces. Place into a bowl, drizzle over a teaspoon of olive oil and season with salt and pepper. Mix well.

* Toast the slices of bread. Once they are golden brown, take the clove of garlic and rub it over one side of each slice of bread.

* Drizzle the remaining olive oil over the bread.

* Now, spoon the tomatoes on top of the toast. Top with fresh basil leaves if you are using them and dive in immediately.

THE MORNING AFTER

SCOTCH PANCAKES WITH BANANA AND MAPLE SYRUP

Serves: 2

Who doesn't love pancakes in the morning? The good news is that these are quick and easy to make. Perfect for brunch on a lazy morning!

65g self-raising flour

Pinch of salt

1 heaped tsp caster sugar

55ml milk

1 medium egg

15g butter, melted, plus a small knob of butter for cooking

1 small banana, sliced, and maple syrup, to serve

* Place the flour, salt and sugar into a bowl and stir them together to combine evenly.

* Measure out the milk into a jug. Crack in the egg and whisk together using a fork. Pour this mixture into the bowl containing the dry ingredients.

* Add the melted butter and stir the mixture together gently until all the flour is mixed in. Don't worry about any lumps.

* Melt the knob of butter in a large frying pan and swirl it around so that the base of the pan is evenly covered in butter. Now, turn the heat up to high so that the pan starts to become quite hot.

* Pour in a couple of dollops of mixture at a time – roughly a tablespoon of mixture for each pancake. Leave the pancakes to cook without touching them for a minute or two until you notice several holes developing on the surface. Now you can flip the pancakes.

* Cook for another couple of minutes on the other side until they are brown on both sides.

* Serve topped with sliced banana and a drizzle of maple syrup.

BANANA, OAT AND HONEY SMOOTHIE

Serves: 1

This creamy breakfast smoothie is super-quick to make and with its helping of oats it will keep you going until lunch.

80ml milk

3 tbsp natural yoghurt

25g porridge oats

1 banana, mashed

1 tbsp honey

* Place all the ingredients into a blender and blitz until smooth. If you don't have a blender, just whisk everything together in a bowl.

* Pour into a glass and drink immediately – this doesn't keep.

BERRY SMOOTHIE

Serves: 1

For those who prefer things fruity, here's an easy way to turn berries into breakfast, fast!

150ml milk

1 small–medium banana, mashed

150g berries of your choice

* Place all the ingredients into a blender and blitz until smooth. If you don't have a blender, just mash the berries, then whisk everything together in a bowl.

* Pour into a glass and drink immediately – this doesn't keep.

Tip: Frozen berries are fine to use here and they are much cheaper than fresh.

CINNAMON FRENCH TOAST

Serves: 2

This is an indulgent weekend breakfast of sweet fried bread, which is very easy to rustle up using just a few simple ingredients.

For the French toast
2 large eggs
1 tsp vanilla extract
60ml double cream
1½ tsp ground cinnamon
2 tsp icing sugar
2 slices of thick white bread or brioche
25g butter

For sprinkling
35g caster sugar
2 tsp ground cinnamon

* Beat the eggs in a bowl. Add the vanilla extract, cream, cinnamon and icing sugar and whisk together well. Pour this mixture into a large shallow bowl.

* Place the slices of bread into the creamy mixture and leave to sit for 3 minutes on each side so the bread soaks up the mixture.

* Once you have turned over the bread to soak on the second side, melt the butter in a large frying pan over a gentle heat.

* Place the slices of bread into the pan, turn up the heat to a medium temperature and cook until the bread is golden on both sides.

* While the bread is cooking, mix the caster sugar and cinnamon together in a small cup. When the bread is done, sprinkle the sugar mixture over each slice and serve immediately.

APPLE BIRCHER MUESLI

Serves: 1

If you want a healthy and filling breakfast to set you up for the day, try Bircher muesli, a mixture of soaked oats and fresh fruit. It's quicker to prepare than porridge and you also get one of your 5-a-day!

60g porridge oats
50ml apple juice
1 eating apple, grated
1 tbsp natural yoghurt
1 tsp honey or maple syrup

Tip: You can also top this with dried fruit and nuts, such as almonds and dried apricots.

* The night before you want to eat this, place the oats and apple juice together in a small bowl. Stir, cover with cling film, and leave in the fridge overnight.

* When you are ready for breakfast, grate an apple onto the juice-soaked oats. Spoon over the yoghurt and pour over the honey or syrup.

* Eat straight away as the apple will brown quickly if left.

VEGGIE FRIED BREAKFAST

Here are some delicious ideas to mix and match for a meat-free morning fry-up! Serve any of the following with vegetarian sausages (cooked as per packet instructions), baked beans and grilled tomatoes. When poaching eggs, make sure to use the freshest eggs possible, so that the whites hold together well; and follow the cooking time given to ensure your yolk remains perfectly runny!

SCRAMBLED EGGS WITH MUSHROOMS

Serves: 1

20g butter

100g mushrooms, cut into chunky pieces

2–3 large eggs, depending on appetite

2 tbsp milk

Salt and pepper

Hot buttered toast, to serve

* Melt half the butter in a saucepan over a medium heat. Add the mushrooms and stir to ensure they become well coated in melted butter.

* Cook for around 15 minutes. Make sure any water from the mushrooms is cooked off.

* While the mushrooms are cooking, crack the eggs into a bowl. Add the milk and season with salt and pepper. Whisk until well combined.

* Melt the remaining butter gently in a non-stick saucepan over a medium heat. Swirl the butter around the pan.

* Pour the egg mixture into the pan and stir continuously until the eggs are scrambled to your liking. For softly scrambled eggs, they'll take about 30 seconds, or for a firmer set, cook for 1 minute. Remove from the heat just before they're cooked to your liking as they will continue to cook in the residual heat of the pan.

* Serve the scrambled eggs on hot buttered toast with the buttery mushrooms on the side.

POACHED EGG ON TOAST

Serves: 1

1 large, very fresh egg
Buttered toast, to serve

* Fill a deep frying pan with water to a depth of 3cm. Place on a high heat and bring to the boil, then crack in the egg, breaking it low over the pan so that it stays in one piece. Turn down the heat and let the egg gently simmer in the water for 4 minutes.

* Carefully scoop out the egg using a slotted spoon. Drain off any excess water then serve the poached egg on hot, buttered toast. It's also delicious on a crumpet or English muffin.

POACHED EGG ON A MUSHROOM

Serves: 1

Small knob of butter
1 large, flat mushroom, such as portobello
1 large very fresh egg
Salt and pepper

* Start by cooking the mushroom. Melt the butter in a small saucepan over a medium heat. Add the mushroom and season with salt and pepper. Cook for 10–15 minutes.

* Meanwhile, fill a deep frying pan with water to a depth of 3cm. Place on a high heat and bring to the boil, then crack in the egg, breaking it low over the pan so that it stays in one piece. Turn down the heat and let the egg gently simmer in the water for 4 minutes.

* Carefully scoop out the egg using a slotted spoon. Drain off any excess water and serve the egg on the hot mushroom.

SAUTÉED POTATOES WITH EGGS AND MUSHROOMS

Serves: 2

4 tbsp olive oil

500g waxy salad potatoes, cut into 2cm cubes

2 large field mushrooms, cut into 1cm thick slices

2 large very fresh eggs

Salt and pepper

* Warm 3 tablespoons of the olive oil in a large saucepan over a medium to high heat. Add the potato cubes and cook for around 10 minutes. The potatoes should start to brown, but not burn.

* After 10 minutes, add the mushrooms and cook for a further 10–15 minutes until the potatoes are tender and the mushrooms are softened.

* Meanwhile, add the final tablespoon of oil to a separate frying pan over a medium heat. Crack the eggs into the frying pan, and cook for around 1½ minutes until the white is set and slightly crispy round the edges.

* Serve the potatoes and mushrooms on plates with the fried eggs on top. Season well with salt and pepper.

FRIED BREAD

Serves: 1

30ml vegetable or sunflower oil

1 slice of bread

Knob of butter (optional)

* Warm the oil in a frying pan over a medium heat.

* Add the bread and cook for 2–3 minutes on each side until crispy and golden.

* If the pan becomes dry, add a little more oil. For a richer flavour, add a knob of butter after you turn the slice.

BREAKFAST BURRITOS

Serves: 1

Roll up, roll up! These warm egg burritos are perfect if you like a bit of spice to wake your tastebuds in the morning. If you prefer your food a bit milder just leave out the jalapeños and hot sauce.

2 large eggs

2 tbsp milk

10g butter

1 tortilla wrap

¼ red peppers, deseeded and finely chopped

1 small tomato, chopped

1 tsp chopped jalapeño peppers

1 tbsp grated mature Cheddar cheese

Hot sauce, to serve (optional)

Salt and pepper

* Crack the eggs into a bowl. Add the milk and season with salt and pepper. Whisk until well combined.

* Melt the butter gently in a non-stick saucepan. Swirl around the pan.

* Pour the egg mixture into the pan over a medium heat. Stir continuously until the eggs are scrambled to your liking. For just-set, softly scrambled eggs, they'll take about 30 seconds, or for a firmer set, cook for 1 minute. Remove from the heat just before they're cooked to your liking as they will continue to cook in the residual heat of the pan.

* Place the tortilla onto a large plate. Transfer the eggs to the centre of the wrap. Add the chopped pepper, tomato and the jalapeños and sprinkle some cheese on top.

* Roll up the tortilla and tuck in the ends to form a burrito.

* Cut in half and eat without delay, with some hot sauce on the side if you like.

CHILLI CORN MUFFINS

Makes: 12 muffins

If you like something savoury in the morning, try these gorgeous cheesy muffins with a chilli kick! They're easy to make, so the hardest thing will be stopping your housemates from gobbling them all up...

250g plain flour

2 tbsp baking powder

Pinch of salt

Pinch of ground paprika

100g sweetcorn

100g Cheddar cheese, grated

Pinch of black pepper

1 red chilli, finely chopped (deseeded if you don't want it too hot)

200ml milk

4 tbsp sunflower oil

2 large eggs

Muffin tray(s)

Paper muffin cases

* Preheat the oven to 180°C Fan/Gas Mark 6. Line a muffin tray with paper muffin cases.

* Sift the plain flour, baking powder, salt and paprika through a sieve into a large mixing bowl. Add the sweetcorn, Cheddar, pepper and chilli and mix in.

* Mix the milk, sunflower oil and eggs together in a jug.

* Pour the wet ingredients into the dry ingredients and stir gently until just combined. Try not to mix too much or the muffins will turn out heavy and dense.

* Distribute the mixture evenly into the muffin cases and bake for around 20 minutes until well risen and golden brown.

* Leave the muffins to cool in the tray for at least 20 minutes after removing from the oven. Then transfer them in their paper cases to a wire rack to cool fully.

* Store in an airtight container and eat within 2–3 days. Once cool, the muffins can be frozen in sealed freezer bags for up to 3 months.

SUMMER BERRY
AND OAT MUFFINS

Makes 12 muffins or 16 fairy cake-sized muffins

Lovely and fruity but not too sweet, these muffins are packed with oats, which makes them substantial enough to stave off any mid-morning hunger pangs.

325g plain flour

1 tbsp baking powder

Pinch of bicarbonate of soda

Pinch of salt

200g light brown soft sugar

50g porridge oats

2 medium eggs

100ml milk

100g natural yoghurt

75ml sunflower oil

1 tsp vanilla extract

125g summer berries (blueberries, raspberries and blackberries are lovely)

Muffin or fairy cake tray(s)

Paper muffin/cake cases

* Preheat the oven to 180°C Fan/Gas Mark 6. Line your muffin tray with the appropriately sized paper cases.

* Sift the flour, baking powder, bicarbonate of soda and salt through a sieve into a large mixing bowl. Add the sugar and oats and stir in.

* Put the eggs, milk, yoghurt, oil and vanilla extract into a jug and whisk together well.

* Pour the wet ingredients into the dry and gently stir to combine. Try not to mix too much or the muffins will turn out heavy and dense. Add the berries and gently stir in to the mixture.

* Divide the muffin mixture evenly among the cake cases and bake for 20–25 minutes for muffins and 15–20 minutes for fairy cakes until golden brown.

* Leave to cool in the tray for at least 20 minutes after removing from the oven. Then transfer the muffins in their paper cases to a wire rack to cool fully.

* Store in an airtight container and eat within 2–3 days. Once cool, the muffins can be frozen in sealed freezer bags for up to 3 months.

BLUEBERRY MUFFINS

Makes 12 muffins or 16 fairy cake-sized muffins

These are the perfect breakfast muffins, full of flavour, but not overly sweet. Bake them on lazy weekend mornings to enjoy while still warm, or whip up a batch at night so that they're ready for a speedy weekday breakfast.

250g plain flour

½ tsp bicarbonate of soda

1 tbsp baking powder

Pinch of salt

125g light brown soft sugar

125g butter, melted

100ml milk

2 medium eggs, beaten

200g fresh blueberries

Muffin or fairy cake tray(s)

Paper muffin/cake cases

Tip: This is a great way to use up any blueberries that have gone squidgy.

* Preheat the oven to 200°C Fan/Gas Mark 7. Line your muffin tray with the appropriately sized paper cases.

* Sift the flour, bicarbonate of soda, baking powder and salt through a sieve into a large mixing bowl. Add the sugar and stir in.

* Pour in the melted butter, milk, beaten eggs and blueberries and stir gently until just combined. Try not to mix too much or the muffins will turn out heavy and dense.

* Divide the mixture evenly among the cake cases and bake for 16–20 minutes for muffins and 12–16 minutes for fairy cakes until well risen and golden brown.

* Leave to cool in the tray for at least 20 minutes after removing from the oven. Then transfer the muffins in their paper cases to a wire rack to cool fully.

* Store in an airtight container and eat within 2–3 days. Once cool, the muffins can be frozen in sealed freezer bags for up to 3 months.

LEMON AND POPPY SEED MUFFINS

Makes: 12 muffins or 16 fairy cake-sized muffins

When it comes to muffin flavours, this is a real classic. The lemon zest balances out the sweetness of the sponge and the poppy seeds add some lovely crunch. They look great too.

225g plain flour
1 tsp bicarbonate of soda
165g light brown soft sugar
Pinch of salt
200ml milk
175ml sunflower
or vegetable oil
1 medium egg, beaten
Finely grated zest of 5 lemons
4 tbsp poppy seeds

Muffin or fairy cake tray(s)
Paper muffin/cake cases

* Preheat the oven to 180°C Fan/Gas Mark 6. Line your muffin tray with the appropriately sized paper cases.

* Sift the flour and bicarbonate of soda through a sieve into a bowl. Add the sugar and salt and stir in.

* Pour the milk, oil and beaten egg into the dry mixture and stir gently to form a sticky batter.

* Add the lemon zest and poppy seeds and stir until just combined. Stop mixing as soon as the flour is incorporated and the seeds are evenly distributed, as over-mixing means the muffins will turn out heavy and dense.

* Spoon the mixture evenly into the cake cases and bake for 25–30 minutes for muffins and 18–22 minutes for fairy cakes until golden brown and well risen.

* Leave to cool in the tray for at least 20 minutes after removing from the oven. Then transfer the muffins in their paper cases to a wire rack to cool fully.

* Store in an airtight container and eat within 2–3 days. Once cool, the muffins can be frozen in sealed freezer bags for up to 3 months.

BANANA CHOC CHIP MUFFINS

Makes: 12 muffins or 16 fairy cake-sized muffins

A great way to use up over-ripe bananas, these lovely moist muffins are studded with chocolate chips and are great for an energy boost to kick off your day.

150g plain flour
1 teaspoon baking powder
½ tsp bicarbonate of soda
3 very ripe bananas
125ml sunflower oil
2 large eggs, beaten
100g caster sugar
150g chocolate chips

Muffin or fairy cake tray(s)
Paper muffin/cake cases

* Preheat the oven to 200°C Fan/Gas Mark 7. Line your muffin tray with the appropriately sized paper cases.

* Sift the flour, baking powder and bicarbonate of soda through a sieve into a large mixing bowl.

* In a medium bowl, mash the bananas well. Then add the oil, beaten eggs and sugar, and mix to combine.

* Pour the banana mixture into the flour and mix very lightly until the flour is only just incorporated. Try not to mix too much or the muffins will turn out heavy and dense.

* Add the chocolate chips and stir in very gently.

* Divide the muffin mixture evenly among the cake cases and bake for 20–25 minutes for muffins and 15–20 minutes for fairy cakes until golden brown.

* Leave to cool in the tin for at least 20 minutes after removing from the oven. Then transfer them in their paper cases to a wire rack to cool fully.

* Store in an airtight container and eat within 2–3 days. Once cool, the muffins can be frozen in sealed freezer bags for up to 3 months.

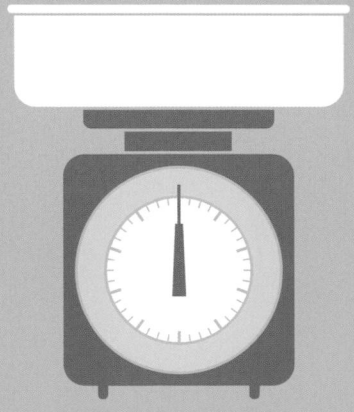

PORRIDGE AND TOPPINGS

Serves: 1

Porridge is one of the most nutritious breakfast options, and also one of the cheapest. Even better, oats really fill you up and help prevent your stomach rumbling mid-lecture! See over the page for plenty of ideas for toppings to make your breakfast even better.

25g porridge oats

4 tbsp milk

4 tbsp water

Your choice of topping (see overleaf)

* Place the oats, milk and water in a saucepan over a medium heat.

* Stir regularly for around 3 minutes until the oats have absorbed much of the liquid.

* Pour the porridge into a bowl and add your choice of topping (see overleaf). You may wish to add another tablespoon of milk to thin your porridge and cool it down if you're in a rush!

PORRIDGE TOPPINGS:

BANANA AND MAPLE SYRUP

Serves: 1

½–1 banana, depending
on appetite

1 tbsp maple syrup, more
if you have a sweet tooth

* Slice the banana thinly onto a bowl of hot porridge.

* Add the syrup, stir together gently and enjoy immediately.

APPLE, SULTANA AND CINNAMON

Serves: 1

1 eating apple, peeled,
cored and cut into small cubes

1 tsp sultanas

1 tsp honey or brown sugar

½ tsp ground cinnamon

* Simply place your hot porridge in a bowl and add the apple chunks, sultanas, sugar or honey and cinnamon.

* Stir well and tuck in.

DATE AND COCONUT

Serves: 1

1 tbsp stoned, chopped dates

1 tbsp desiccated coconut

1 tsp sugar or honey

* Add the dates, coconut and sugar or honey to a bowl of hot porridge.

* Stir well and enjoy immediately.

CHOCOLATE

Serves: 1

3–4 squares of chocolate,
chopped

1 tsp sugar or honey

* Add the chopped chocolate and sugar or honey to a bowl of hot porridge.

* Stir well. The chocolate should melt in the hot porridge. Eat straight away.

CINNAMON AND RAISIN

Serves: 1

1–2 tsp ground cinnamon,
to taste

1 tsp raisins

1 tsp sugar or honey

* Add the cinnamon, raisins and sugar or honey to a bowl of hot porridge.

* Mix well and eat straight away.

MANGO AND COCONUT MILK

Serves: 1

½ fresh mango, cut into chunks

2 tbsp coconut milk

1 tsp sugar or honey

* Add the mango, coconut milk and sugar or honey to a bowl of hot porridge.

* Mix well and eat straight away.

GREEK YOGHURT AND HONEY

Serves: 1

2 tbsp Greek yoghurt

2 tsp honey

* Add the yoghurt and honey to a bowl of hot porridge.

* Stir well and enjoy immediately.

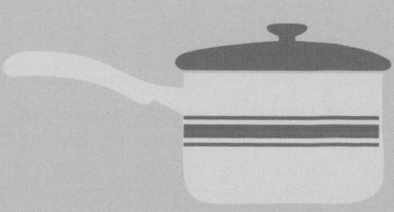

SWEETS

CHOCOLATE FUDGE BROWNIES

Makes: a tray of 12–14 brownies

Dark, dense and squidgy, these brownies taste even better a day or two after baking. Use the best-quality chocolate you can afford as it makes all the difference here. You can even serve them warm with ice cream for pudding.

190g dark chocolate,
broken into squares

125g salted butter, plus extra
for greasing

1 tsp instant coffee powder

250g caster sugar

3 large eggs, beaten

60g self-raising flour

1 tsp cocoa powder

20cm square cake tin
Non-stick baking paper

Tip: These brownies also make a great sundae, topped with ice cream, sauce and nuts.

* Preheat the oven to 180°C Fan/Gas Mark 6. Grease a 20cm square cake tin and line with non-stick baking paper.

* Melt the chocolate and butter together. You can do this in the microwave (make sure you check it every 20 seconds so that it does not burn) or in a heatproof bowl over a small saucepan of simmering water (stir frequently and check the water isn't actually in contact with the bottom of the bowl).

* When the chocolate and butter are melted, mix vigorously to combine the two. Add the coffee powder, stir again and leave to cool for 10 minutes or so.

* Add the sugar to the chocolate mixture once it has cooled a little, followed by the eggs.

* Add the flour and cocoa powder and gently stir in.

* Pour the mixture into the prepared tin and bake for 35–40 minutes until the top has a shiny crust. Be careful not to overcook, as the brownies will solidify as they cool – you want them to stay nice and fudgy in the middle.

* Allow to cool completely in the tin before slicing up. (When slicing, cut carefully so as not to scratch the tin.)

* Store in an airtight container and eat within 7 days.

WHITE CHOCOLATE CHIP COOKIES

Makes: 8–10 large cookies

Soft, chewy and sweet, these cookies are amazing eaten fresh from the oven. If you're new to baking, this is a great place to start and will make you very popular with friends and housemates.

Vegetable oil or butter,
for greasing
110g butter, softened
200g light brown soft sugar
1 tsp vanilla extract
1 large egg, beaten
200g plain flour
125g white chocolate chips

Two large baking sheets
Non-stick baking paper

* Preheat the oven to 160°C Fan/Gas Mark 4. Grease two large baking sheets well and line with non-stick baking paper.

* In a large mixing bowl, beat together the butter, sugar and vanilla extract with a wooden spoon or electric mixer until well combined, fluffy and pale in colour.

* Add the beaten egg to the mixture, a little at a time, mixing well after each addition until completely combined.

* Sift in the flour through a sieve, then stir in gently until completely incorporated. Stir in the chocolate chips so that they are evenly distributed. The mixture will be soft and thick.

* Place mounds of the mixture onto the prepared baking sheets, allowing a tablespoonful of mixture per cookie, and spacing them well apart as the cookies will expand while cooking.

* Bake in the oven for 10–12 minutes until they are lightly golden.

* Leave to cool on the sheets for 20 minutes, during which time they will firm up, before transferring to a wire rack to cool entirely. (Or you can eat them while still a little warm, but make sure they have had the first 20 minutes to cool or the chocolate will burn your mouth.)

* Store in an airtight container and eat within 7 days.

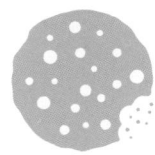

QUICK TIRAMISU

Serves: 4–6

This creamy, coffee-flavoured treat is really simple to put together.
If possible, make it a day in advance and leave in the fridge for the
flavours to intensify. If you already have a bottle of Tia Maria this is
a great use for it, otherwise pick up a small one and save the rest for
cocktails (or pop a sneaky shot into a coffee!).

200g sponge fingers
300ml strong coffee, cooled
120ml Tia Maria
400g ready-made custard
250g mascarpone cheese
300ml double cream
2 tbsp cocoa powder, to dust

* Lay out the sponge fingers in a large bowl or serving dish.
  It needs to be about 1.5 litres in capacity.

* In a jug, mix the coffee and Tia Maria together and pour over
  the sponge fingers, so that they are well covered in the liquid.

* Put the custard and mascarpone in a bowl and beat together
  well. Pour evenly over the sponge fingers.

* Whisk the double cream until it is thickly whipped and stiff,
  and spoon it over the custard and mascarpone layer.

* Cover with cling film and chill in the fridge for as long as you
  can before serving – overnight is ideal.

* Dust with cocoa powder and serve

CHOCOCCINO MUFFINS

Makes: 12 muffins

Inspired by everyone's favourite hot drink, these gorgeous muffins are flavoured with coffee and studded with chocolate chunks. What better excuse to take a break from revision or essays?!

325g self-raising flour

150g caster sugar

1–2 tbsp espresso powder (depending on how strong you like the coffee flavour to be)

1 large egg

250ml milk

80g butter, melted

100g milk chocolate, chopped into chunks

Muffin tray(s)
Paper muffin cases

* Preheat the oven to 180°C Fan/Gas Mark 6. Line your muffin tray with paper muffin cases.

* Mix the flour, sugar and espresso powder together in a large mixing bowl.

* Whisk the egg, milk and melted butter together in a jug.

* Pour the wet ingredients into the dry ingredients, add the chocolate chunks, and stir very gently until just combined. Be careful not to overmix as this can cause the muffins to turn out dense and heavy.

* Distribute the mixture evenly into the cases and bake for around 20 minutes until well risen and firm to the touch.

* Allow the muffins to cool in the tray for 20 minutes before transferring, in their paper cases, to a wire rack to cool fully.

* Store in an airtight container and eat within 3–5 days. Once cool, the muffins can be frozen in sealed freezer bags for up to 3 months.

NO-BAKE CHOCOLATE TIFFIN

Makes: 8–10 bars

Tiffin is a gorgeous mixture of chocolate and crushed biscuits.
It's super-simple to make and doesn't even need the oven!
Once cut into bars, it keeps really well in an airtight box.

200g chocolate
(use milk or dark,
whichever you prefer)

100g butter, plus extra
for greasing

2 tbsp golden syrup

225g digestive biscuits

80g glacé cherries

50g white chocolate chunks

20cm square cake tin
Non-stick baking paper

* Grease a 20cm square cake tin and line with non-stick baking paper. Set aside.

* Melt the chocolate, butter and golden syrup together in a bowl. You can do this in the microwave (make sure you check it every 20 seconds so that it does not burn) or in a heatproof bowl over a small pan of simmering water.

* When the chocolate, butter and syrup are melted, mix vigorously to combine.

* Place the biscuits in a plastic freezer bag, flatten to remove as much air as possible and knot the top. Bash with a rolling pin or similar implement until the biscuits are broken up into small pieces. Don't use anything sharp that might pierce the bag.

* Place the biscuit pieces, cherries and chocolate chunks into a large mixing bowl.

* Pour the melted chocolate mixture into the bowl and mix well to coat the dry ingredients in chocolate.

* Tip the mixture into the prepared tin, cover with cling film and chill for at least 3 hours.

* When the mixture has chilled thoroughly, it will be very firm. You will be able to remove it from the tin in one block and slice into bars.

* The bars will be ready to go now, but will also keep for up to a week in a tin or plastic box.

CRANBERRY AND PECAN FLAPJACKS

Makes: 12 flapjacks

Flapjacks are a brilliant snack to keep in your cupboard in case of emergencies! They're full of energy, so are great for taking in your bag to see you through a long day or night in the library. The pecans make these very special, but feel free to use cheaper nuts if you're on a tight budget.

200g butter, plus extra
for greasing
175g light brown soft sugar
150g golden syrup
300g porridge oats
150g dried cranberries
100g pecan halves

20cm square cake tin
Non-stick baking paper

Tip: Vary the fruit and nuts in these flapjacks according to your taste and budget. Sultanas, prunes, dates and desiccated coconut are all great additions.

* Preheat the oven to 150°C Fan/Gas Mark 3. Grease a 20cm square cake tin and line with non-stick baking paper.

* Melt the butter, sugar and syrup together in a saucepan over a low heat.

* Add the oats, cranberries and pecans and stir well into the melted mixture, ensuring all the oats are covered in the liquid.

* Carefully transfer the mixture to the prepared tin. Spread out evenly and level the top.

* Bake the flapjack for 20–25 minutes until the edges have started to brown a little. Don't worry if there appears to be some excess butter on the top.

* As soon as the flapjack comes out of the oven, cut into slices in the tin, cutting right down to the base and being careful not to scratch the tin. (This initial cutting is important because as the flapjack cools it becomes very firm and more difficult to cut.)

* Leave to cool and firm up in the tin for an hour, then use the baking paper to lift the whole flapjack out of the tin. Peel off the paper and place the flapjack on a wire rack to cool fully. Once cool, use a sharp knife to go over the initial cuts again, then separate the pieces.

* Store in an airtight container and eat within 7 days.

LEMON NO-BAKE CHEESECAKE

Serves: 8–10 people

Light, zesty and extremely moreish, this gorgeous cheesecake is super-simple to make, and doesn't even require the oven!

For the base
12 digestive biscuits

80g butter, melted,
plus extra for greasing

For the topping
225g full-fat cream cheese

400g can of sweetened
condensed milk

300ml double cream

Juice and finely grated zest
of 2 unwaxed lemons

20cm round springform
cake tin

* Lightly grease a 20cm springform cake tin and set aside.

* Start by making the base. Place the biscuits in a plastic freezer bag, flatten to remove as much air as possible and knot the top. Bash with a rolling pin or similar implement until the biscuits are reduced to crumbs. Don't use anything sharp that might pierce the bag.

* Empty the biscuit crumbs into a mixing bowl and stir in the melted butter. Tip this mixture into your prepared tin and flatten down evenly to cover the base of the tin. Set aside.

* Place the cream cheese and condensed milk in a large bowl and beat well with a wooden spoon or electric mixer.

* In another large bowl, whip the cream vigorously (an electric whisk or mixer helps here) until it becomes much thicker and can be lifted into peaks, then add it to the cream cheese mixture and stir in very gently.

* Finally, add the lemon juice and most of the zest (save a little for decoration) and gently mix in.

* Carefully spoon the cheesecake mixture into the tin over the biscuit base and smooth out the top. Scatter with the reserved lemon zest. Chill in the fridge for at least 4 hours, or ideally overnight, before serving.

BAKED CHOCOLATE BANANAS

Serves: 2

Once you've discovered these, there's no going back! Simply pop the wrapped bananas in the oven and – hey presto! – warm, chocolatey treats just waiting to be unwrapped. The texture of the banana becomes soft and creamy, a bit like custard. They are also brilliant on the barbecue – cook the wrapped bananas directly on the coals.

2 large bananas, skin on

6 squares of chocolate (either milk or dark)

* Preheat the oven to 150°C Fan/Gas Mark 2.

* Keeping the skin on, take your bananas and cut a deep slit lengthways down each one. Place the squares of chocolate in the slit. Wrap tightly in foil and place in an ovenproof dish, keeping the side with the chocolate facing upwards.

* Bake the bananas for around 20–30 minutes until very soft and the chocolate is melted. Don't worry if the skins turn black, this is normal!

* Unwrap and eat immediately with a spoon.

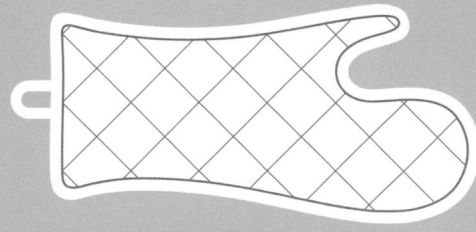

STICKY TOFFEE PUDDING

Serves: 6–8

This fantastically sweet British pudding is a cinch to make yourself, and your friends are bound to love you for it.

For the pudding

150g dates,
stoned and chopped

1 tsp bicarbonate of soda

275ml boiling water

40g butter, softened

150g caster sugar

2 medium eggs, beaten

1 tsp vanilla extract

150g self-raising flour

For the sauce

275ml double cream

1 tbsp treacle

50g dark brown soft sugar

* Place the dates into a heatproof bowl. Add the bicarbonate of soda and pour over the boiling water. Leave the dates to soften for at least an hour (or overnight if time allows).

* Preheat the oven to 180°C Fan/Gas Mark 6.

* In a large mixing bowl, beat together the butter and sugar with a wooden spoon or electric mixer until pale and fluffy. This will take a few minutes as there is quite a lot of sugar.

* Add the beaten eggs, a little at a time, beating well after each addition. Add the vanilla extract too, and stir in.

* Sift in the flour through a sieve and stir well.
  Now, tip in the dates and their liquid.

* Transfer the mixture into a 1.5-litre ovenproof dish.
  Bake for 30–35 minutes until firm.

* To make the sauce, put the cream, treacle and brown sugar together in a saucepan over a medium heat. Stir together well and allow the mixture to bubble for around 10 minutes. Preheat the grill to a high temperature.

* Once the pudding is cooked, pour over the sauce and place under the grill until it bubbles slightly around the edge, taking care that the topping does not brown.

* Remove from the grill, cut up the pudding into portions and serve, ideally with vanilla ice cream.

BANANA AND CHOCOLATE CHIP LOAF CAKE

Serves: 8

This easy loaf is a great way to use up any bananas that are too ripe to eat. The chocolate chips turn it into an indulgent treat. It's lovely eaten while still slightly warm.

Vegetable oil or butter, for greasing

250g very ripe bananas (approx. 2 large ones)

2 large eggs

250g caster sugar

1 tsp vanilla extract

50g salted butter, very soft

250g self-raising flour

1 tsp bicarbonate of soda

150g dark chocolate chips or chopped dark chocolate

900g loaf tin

Non-stick baking paper

Tip: When using chocolate chips, it can often work out better value to buy bar of good-quality chocolate and chop it up into small chunks. Bars tend to be better quality than chips and you get more more for your money.

* Preheat the oven to 180°C Fan/Gas Mark 6.

* Grease a 900g loaf tin and line with non-stick baking paper.

* In a large bowl, mash the bananas well. Whisk in the eggs, sugar and vanilla extract.

* Add the butter and beat in vigorously with a wooden spoon or electric mixer until the ingredients are well combined.

* Sift the flour and bicarbonate of soda through a sieve into the bowl and stir in gently.

* Finally, gently stir in the chocolate chips or chunks.

* Transfer the mixture into the prepared tin and bake for 45 minutes–1 hour until risen and golden brown, and a skewer or cocktail stick inserted into the centre comes out clean. If it doesn't, return the cake to the oven for another 5 minutes and then test again.

* Leave to cool in the tin for 20 minutes before turning out and allowing to cool fully on a wire rack.

* Store in an airtight container and eat within 3–5 days. Once cool, the cake can be frozen in a sealed freezer bag for up to 3 months.

CHOCOLATE RED WINE CAKE

Makes: 1 large cake

This delicious cake manages to taste of chocolate, fruit and spice all at once. It's excellent as a dessert with cream or crème fraîche, and equally good with a cup of tea in the afternoon. Be aware that not all wine is suitable for vegetarians (see page 14), so check the label or the winemaker's website to be absolutely sure.

250g butter, softened,
plus extra for greasing

250g caster sugar

1 tsp vanilla extract

4 large eggs, beaten

4 tsp cocoa powder

1 tsp ground cinnamon

Pinch of salt

250g self-raising flour

125ml red wine

125g dark (70% cocoa)
chocolate, melted and cooled
(see page 196 for melting
instructions)

20cm round cake tin

Non-stick baking paper

* Preheat the oven to 180°C Fan/Gas Mark 6.

* Grease a 20cm round cake tin and line with non-stick baking paper. Set aside.

* In a large mixing bowl, beat together the butter and sugar with a wooden spoon or electric mixer, until pale and fluffy.

* Stir the vanilla extract into the beaten egg and then add this to the butter and sugar mixture a little at a time, beating well after every addition.

* Sift in the cocoa, cinnamon, salt and self-raising flour through a sieve. Gently stir into the wet mixture.

* Pour in the red wine gradually, mixing well. Finally, pour in the melted chocolate and stir gently to ensure all ingredients are well combined.

* Transfer the mixture to the prepared tin and bake in the oven for 45-55 minutes until risen and cooked through. Test after 45 minutes by inserting a skewer or cocktail stick into the centre. If it comes out clean, the cake is cooked. If some liquid mixture sticks to the cocktail stick, it's not yet ready, so return it to the oven for another 5 minutes and then test again.

* When cooked, remove the cake from the oven and allow to cool in the tin for 15 minutes. Then remove from the tin and place on a wire rack to cool fully before slicing.

* Store in an airtight container and eat within 3–5 days. Once cool, the can be frozen in a sealed freezer bag for up to 3 months.

APPLE AND CINNAMON STRUDEL

Serves: 6

This traditional Austrian pud is the ultimate winter comfort food. It's the perfect follow-up to a Sunday lunch, and bound to warm your cockles. Serve hot with cream or ice cream.

5 small eating apples, peeled, cored and cut into 1cm cubes

Juice of ½ lemon

2 tsp ground cinnamon

150g light brown soft sugar

Vegetable oil or butter, for greasing

200g ready-rolled puff pastry, fridge-cold

2 tsp milk

Large baking sheet
Non-stick baking paper

* Preheat the oven to 180°C Fan/Gas Mark 6.

* Place the apple cubes, lemon juice, cinnamon and sugar in a bowl and stir together well. Set aside.

* Grease a large baking sheet well and line with non-stick baking paper. Lay out the sheet of puff pastry carefully on it.

* Spoon out the apple mixture along one edge of the pastry, running about 3cm away from the edge.

* Once you have created an even line of fruit along the pastry, tightly roll up the pastry from one of the long sides, with the fruit in the centre, like a Swiss roll.

* Once you have rolled up the pastry, squeeze it together gently and press down on the seam to make sure it is sealed. Fold up the ends well and press together to seal.

* Arrange the strudel so the pastry seam is underneath. Brush with milk and make a few slits in the pastry on the top.

* Bake for 25–30 minutes until the pastry is golden brown and crisp. Serve warm or cold, with cream or ice cream.

PLUM AND CINNAMON CRUMBLE

Serves: 4

A classic fruit crumble is one of the cheapest and simplest puds you can make and ideal for feeding a crowd, perhaps to round off a hearty Sunday lunch.

600g plums, halved and stones removed

2 tsp ground cinnamon

130g plain flour

140g unsalted butter, chilled and cubed

40g caster sugar

40g demerara sugar

50g rolled oats

* Preheat the oven to 200°C Fan/Gas Mark 7.

* Place the halved plums in the bottom of a medium-sized ovenproof dish. Sprinkle the cinnamon evenly over the plums and set aside.

* Sift the flour through a sieve into a large mixing bowl. Add the cold butter cubes and rub them into the flour using your fingertips until the mixture looks like breadcrumbs.

* Add both types of sugar and the oats and mix through evenly.

* Tip the crumble mixture on top of the plums in the baking dish and make sure they are evenly covered, right to the edges. You should have enough topping to form a generous layer over the fruit.

* Bake for 30–40 minutes until the crumble topping is golden brown and the fruit is cooked through and bubbling up the sides. Serve hot with cream, ice cream or custard.

Tip: If you like your crumble very sweet, sprinkle a tablespoon of caster sugar over the plums before adding the crumble topping. The sweetness also depends on the fruit as some plums can be sharper than others. If in doubt, try a little bit of uncooked plum before adding sugar.

APPLE CRISP PUDDING

Serves: 4–6

A bit like a fruit crumble, but with a bread topping, this is very easy and cheap to make, and is a great way to use up stale bread. It's equally good eaten hot or cold.

4 eating apples, peeled, cored and sliced

50g light brown soft sugar

8 slices stale white bread, crusts removed and cut into squares

60g caster sugar

110g butter, melted

2 tsp ground cinnamon

Pinch of ground cloves

* Preheat the oven to 170°C Fan/Gas Mark 5.

* Place the apples into an ovenproof dish and sprinkle with the light brown soft sugar.

* Take your squares of bread and layer them attractively over the top of the apples.

* Add the caster sugar to the melted butter, along with the cinnamon and cloves, and whisk together well.

* Drizzle the butter evenly over the bread so that it is all covered.

* Bake for 40–45 minutes until the bread is golden brown and the apples are soft. Serve hot or cold.

BAKED COCONUT
RICE PUDDING

Serves: 6

This is a soft and creamy pudding with a gentle coconut flavour.
Keep leftovers for up to 3 days in the fridge; they can be reheated on
a low heat in a saucepan or in the microwave, or are delicious cold.
Make sure to buy proper pudding rice as other types don't work here.

Knob of butter, for greasing

400ml can coconut milk

725ml full-fat milk

75ml double cream

125g caster sugar

250g pudding rice

Jam of your choice,
to serve (optional)

* Preheat the oven to 140°C Fan/Gas Mark 3.

* Grease a 1-litre capacity ovenproof dish well with butter so
  that the rice won't stick.

* Whisk the coconut milk, milk and cream together in a large
  mixing jug. Add the sugar and rice and stir well.

* Pour into the dish and stir once more.

* Bake for 80–90 minutes until the rice is cooked through.
  Serve with your favourite jam on the side.

LEMON VODKA SORBET

Serves: 4–6 (Vegan)

For a more sophisticated take on vodka jelly, try this zesty vodka sorbet! It makes a very refreshing dessert, or you could even pop a small scoop of sorbet into a cocktail in place of ice cubes.

250g caster sugar
250ml lemon juice
45ml vodka

* Put 300ml water, the sugar, lemon juice and vodka in a saucepan and dissolve the sugar by stirring constantly while bringing the mixture to boiling point.

* Once the sugar has dissolved, remove from the heat and allow to cool until it is room temperature.

* Pour the mixture into a plastic container and put into the freezer.

* Remove the mixture from the freezer after 1 hour and whisk with an electric mixer to break up the ice crystals, then return to the freezer. Repeat this step three times.

* After the sorbet has been whisked for the third time, return to the freezer for a few more hours to freeze solid. Leave it there until you are ready to eat.

COCONUT AND LIME ICE CREAM

Serves: 4–6

Why splash the cash on a tub of premium ice cream when you can make your own? This easy recipe doesn't require an ice-cream machine – all you need is an electric whisk. Keep a tub of this tropical treat in the freezer for whenever you need something sweet.

300ml double cream

400ml can of coconut milk

120g caster sugar

**Grated zest and juice
of 2 large limes**

* Place all the ingredients together into a large saucepan over a medium heat. Gently bring up to the boil, stirring constantly to dissolve the sugar.

* Once the sugar has dissolved, remove from the heat and allow to cool to room temperature.

* Pour the mixture into a plastic container with a lid. Make sure you use a large plastic box as the mixture will increase in volume. Put in the freezer for an hour.

* Remove the mixture from the freezer after 1 hour and whisk with an electric whisk to break up the ice crystals, then return to the freezer. Repeat this step three times. It will increase in volume after whisking for the first time.

* After the ice cream has been whisked for the third time, return to the freezer for a few more hours to freeze solid. Leave it there until you are ready to eat.

INDEX

Page numbers in **bold** denote an illustration

AUTHOR'S ACKNOWLEDGEMENTS

Thank you to my fantastic agent, Clare Hulton, for seeing something in me, and for all your support, guidance and answers to my numerous questions.

Sincerest thanks to Jenny Heller at Quercus for your vision, enthusiasm and backing. It is a great pleasure and privilege to work with you. Thank you to Ione Walder for so expertly guiding me through every step and for being a complete and utter joy to work with, and thanks indeed to everyone at Quercus for all your hard work. Caroline and Clive at Harris + Wilson, Jonathan Cherry and Lincoln Jefferson, thank you for a brilliant photo shoot, and for being such fun to work with. Thanks also to A-Side studio for your great design and layout.

Many thanks are due to every single member of my testing team for going above and beyond to triple-test each recipe. I'm also lucky to have so many wonderful friends who haven't forgotten me despite how elusive I've been over the last couple of years. Thanks for sticking with me and for your constant support. Thank you to Philippa Wadsworth for all your time and advice, and to Alexandra Wilby, Judith Arkle and Claire Reid for kindly allowing me to adapt your recipes.

Thank you to all my family for your support and encouragement. Particular thanks to Claire Crook for all your help testing recipes, and to Louise Martin for being there from day one. I thank you for all those long days spent in the kitchen and for keeping me smiling amidst the chaos. Special thanks to Jean Harker for your time, generosity, wisdom and advice. Thank you to my wonderful sister, Lucy, for absolutely everything. I know I ask you for a lot of help. Thanks too, to Andy for being awesome.

I couldn't do what I do now without the never-ending support and generosity of my parents. Although I am supposed to be grown up, I really could not manage without everything you do for me, so thank you. Finally, thank you to Tony, for everything.

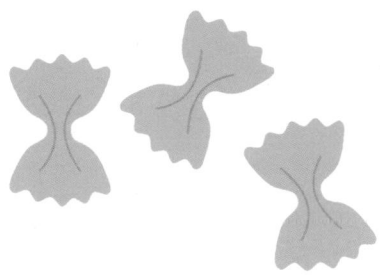

Quercus Editions Ltd
Carmelite House
50 Victoria Embankment
London
EC4Y 0DZ

First published in 2013

A catalogue record of this book is available from the British Library

ISBN 978 1 78206 008 6

Publishing Director: Jenny Heller
Project Editor: Ione Walder
Produced by: Harris + Wilson
Design: A-Side Studio
Food styling: Lincoln Jefferson

Printed and bound in China

10 9 8 7 6 5 4 3 2